MORE PRAISE FOR THE BIPOLAR ADDICT

Conor Bezane sees through the darkness with startling clarity in this powerful, unsentimental journal of descent into madness and back again. A tightly-wound memoir, the author's economy of words pays dividends time after time, the stench of crack pipes as viscerally conveyed as the ecstasy of teenage punk rock catharsis. Singing like an anthem for the "dually diagnosed," The Bipolar Addict is a porch light left on at night for those seeking shelter from the storm and against relentless headwinds trying to find their way back home again.

— Jim Fraenkel, former VP, MTV News

In his unflinching memoir, Conor Bezane chronicles his struggles with bipolar disorder and addiction. The stories he tells are harrowing yet hopeful as he offers a rare glimpse into the mind of someone who turns to alcohol and drugs in a desperate — yet all too common — attempt to soothe a chemically misfiring brain. A must-read for people grappling with the double whammy of a mood disorder coupled with addiction — and those who love them.

— Betsy Forhan, Executive Producer,
National Geographic Channel

With The Bipolar Addict, *Conor Bezane fearlessly opens up about his personal demons, delivering a moving and unique memoir that recounts not only his own harrowing and deeply personal odyssey to sobriety, but celebrates, in vivid detail, the triumphs of others in recovery. The book both inspires and consoles while making a percipient argument for temperance.*

— Chris Harris, True Crime
and Pop Culture Journalist

THE
BIPOLAR
ADDICT

THE
BIPOLAR
ADDICT

DRINKS, DRUGS, DELIRIUM & WHY SOBER IS THE NEW COOL

CONOR BEZANE

We are the music-makers, and we are the dreamers of dreams.
—Arthur O'Shaughnessy, 19th-century poet,
as quoted by Willy Wonka

DISCLAIMER

The Bipolar Addict is part-memoir and not intended to be a guide of any kind. It reflects the author's present recollections of experiences over time. Some dialogue has been recreated, and some names and identifying details have been changed to protect the privacy of individuals. People interviewed in the book were sober at the time of interview.

The content is not intended to be a substitute for professional medical advice, diagnosis, or treatment. Always seek the advice of your physician or other qualified health provider with any questions you may have regarding a medical condition. Never disregard professional medical advice or delay in seeking it because of something you have read in this book.

If you think you may have a medical emergency, call your doctor or 911 or local emergency number immediately. *The Bipolar Addict* and the author do not recommend or endorse any specific tests, physicians, products, procedures, opinions, or other information that may be mentioned in the book. Reliance on any information provided by the book is solely at your own risk.

CONTENTS

PART III: THE WORLD OF RECOVERY

INTRODUCTION

This Is Your Bipolar Brain on Drugs:
What Bipolar Addiction Feels Like

It's the feeling you get when you're higher than the moon for no reason at all. You're invincible. Everything you do or say is brilliant. You're hyper-aware. You're bathing in a pool of euphoria. Everyone's your friend. People are attracted to your über-positive energy. You go on shopping sprees. Life is magical.

When you're manic, you're in a heightened mood marked by delusions of grandeur and sometimes psychosis and hallucinations. It's like being under the influence, but instead of being influenced by a foreign substance, you're simply at the whim of your own brain. You think you're just happy, that everything is going your way and you don't have a problem. But you do.

You're high. But you didn't do any drugs. That high is addictive. But now you just want to get higher. So you smoke some weed,

1

snort some coke, drink some vodka, pop some Vicodin, do some ketamine. You speedball. You candyflip. You smoke crack. Anything to get you higher and higher. And then you get addicted. This is bipolar addiction.

* * *

There are 5.7 million people living with bipolar in the U.S.; 60 percent of them are clinical addicts. The bipolar addict needs no occasion to get drunk or high. It's not a weekend thing. It's not a New Year's Eve thing or a wedding thing. It's an everyday thing. Simply being at home alone is the perfect occasion.

The addiction continues when the coin is flipped and mania turns to depression. Now that you're on the downslide, you'll do anything to regain the euphoria you lost, or just make yourself feel slightly better than the agony brought on by the crushing blackness swallowing you. You're locked away in a dungeon of despair. Weed might help. Even though alcohol doesn't, because it's a depressant, many of the un-sober among us use it anyway to alter our state of mind.

No surprise: Depression sucks. Your body feels heavy. You cry every day, sometimes hysterically, sometimes sobbing. You can feel the depression in your bones. They ache with anguish. A heaviness weighs upon your brain.

Your medication cocktail doesn't work when you drink and do drugs every day. But you still feel good because you're high. Maybe you're not manic, but you're definitely not happy either. In reality, you're miserable.

You're that hamster on a wheel chasing the mania. And it feels good.

Until you lose it at the office — then lose your job. Or embarrass yourself in public to the point the authorities are called. Or attempt suicide.

Then you go to rehab and learn what it feels like to be a normal human being again. You get sober one day at a time. Your medication starts to work again. Maybe you go back to school. You get your career on track again. And you feel better than ever.

* * *

When I was first diagnosed with bipolar, it was only shortly after the condition had begun losing its original stigma, having once been known as "manic depression." The connection between addiction and bipolar was only just being explored. Few of us dually diagnosed even knew how common our condition was, and even fewer friends and family were aware of what we'd gone through — and what we continue to go through even after we've undergone years of help and come out alive on the other end.

In rehab, the only resource I had was my group and my mentor. And although I credit them with getting me through those first dark days, their journeys were vastly different from mine, because they were "only" battling addiction, which in itself is a nightmare I wouldn't wish on anyone.

But when you're dually diagnosed, you're waging two separate wars at once — and each requires different weapons. You can't use the same strategy with one as you do with the other. And even if you gain ground in one battle, a minor setback in the other could cause you to slip backward in both.

Of course, I didn't understand all that at the time. It's only with hindsight that I can see how much easier my own journey to recovery would have been had I only been armed with the knowledge of my true condition.

So once I recovered, I wrote the book I wish I'd had when I received my dual diagnosis, the book I wanted to read when I decided to get sober.

I wrote it with the hope that it would provide if not a roadmap for recovery then a source of hope and inspiration for the dually diagnosed. I also hope it allows others like me to feel part of something bigger, rather than feel isolated and alone.

The stories in this book are meant to be both inspirational and cautionary. I like to think of *The Bipolar Addict* as an informational resource for family members and friends of the afflicted — or anyone who wants to learn more about mental illness and how it manifests.

Part One is my personal memoir, followed by the real-life stories of five other "Eccentrics," as I like to refer to the creative and idiosyncratic individuals who have been dually diagnosed. (It should be noted that these interview subjects were easy to find, which is testament to how addiction and mental illness simultaneously take hold of so many people.) I hope to let others like us know that they are not alone — that we too have gone through this hell and lived to see a brighter day. Although I interviewed numerous dually diagnosed individuals, I chose to include those I felt showcased the more common tendencies, as well as individuals whose stories were so over the top they make most others pale in comparison — which could help your obstacles seem suddenly far more manageable.

To close, I chose to end as the seminal *Alcoholics Anonymous* begins, with insight from a medical professional.

As dark as our stories sometimes get, we Eccentrics somehow manage to find the light more often than not. It is that symbol of hope and strength that I hope you take with you when you're done with this book.

PART I

MANIC
TELEVISION

I became insane, with long intervals of horrible sanity.
— bipolar poet Edgar Allan Poe

CHAPTER 1

KISS AND TELL

January 2012

'm sitting in an alley in downtown Chicago at 3AM smoking crack with Rashaad, a homeless guy who, although we've just met, instinctively knows I'm gay. We're chain-smoking Newports and drinking a super-size can of Earthquake malt liquor in between hits from his crack pipe. It's below freezing out. Dumpsters all around. The stench of garbage. Graffiti on brick walls — tags, not pieces.

Rashaad admires my footwear — black Ted Baker London shoes. He wants me to step on his hand with all my might. He's easily twenty years my senior, a Vietnam vet who readily confesses he enjoys pain. "Walk on me," he commands. Not a suggestion, an order. I do it. I've always been a people pleaser.

"Have you ever kissed a black man before?"

"No," I say. Without pause, he leans over and kisses me. I'm so high that I don't hesitate to kiss him back.

As we're swapping saliva, I can tell he's an inexperienced kisser. He inserts his tongue deep in my mouth and moves it around, not delicately but aggressively. It's a bad, sloppy kiss. Despite how awkward and unpleasurable the situation is, I let it go on for a good half minute, unable to find a polite way to extricate myself.

After the kiss, Rashaad invites himself over to my apartment. That's where I draw the line. At least there's some sanity left in me. I feign fatigue and leave shortly after. I never see him again.

* * *

I've been drinking every single day for the past five years. At this point, I'm rather certain I could outdrink *Kill 'Em All*–era James Hetfield of Metallica, a band whose consumption was so legendary in the '80s that it earned the name Alcoholica. I'm also on seven different drugs for my bipolar disorder.

My experience with recreational drugs is different from that of the normies (as those of us with mental illness often refer to the chemically stable members of society): Uppers bring me down and downers bring me up. That's just how the drug-abusing experience is for me.

Mixing recreational drugs with prescription pills is dangerous. I know better. But I'm living dangerously and I don't care. Getting high has replaced all the career goals that once drove me. It's my daily purpose, and I don't let anything get in my way.

I live in downtown Chicago in the upscale neighborhood of River North, where I moved in 2009 after getting laid off the year prior from my corporate-yet-creative job as a producer for MTV News in New York. In less than a year I'd spent all my severance on beer and wine and was forced to move back to the city where I grew up and where my parents still kept an apartment even though they'd retired to Hawaii. The apartment is riddled with artifacts from my childhood: family pictures, the same art that's hung on the walls since my grade-school years, the same furniture since I left for college.

I'm lucky I have a place to go. In fact, I'm kind of a spoiled brat — my parents are subsidizing my life, with the caveat that it lasts only "until I find a full-time job." The job hunting has taken a backseat to my drinking — I haven't even submitted a resume since I moved back to Chicago three years ago — making me a career alcoholic living rent-free on Mom and Dad's dime. Thanks to the Great Recession and the media industry's subsequent nosedive, I have a ready-made excuse for being unemployed.

I'm drinking two six-packs or two bottles of wine every night. Sometimes I even go out late to scavenge for a third six-pack. The recycling bin on my floor of the building is perpetually chock-full of empty bottles of Blue Moon, my poison of choice.

I long for the mania that so often comes with being bipolar, and being drunk feels almost like it. Mania can be fun — at least for a short time. But after a few months, it can get downright scary. You hear and see things that aren't there. Take the worst paranoia you've ever experienced, multiply it by a thousand, and you're still not even close. When you're manic, you're in a fantasyland, but one that exudes only darkness.

I've long passed the enjoyable stage of mania and have moved on to the next: isolation. Rare is the day I see another soul, except for the clerks at the handful of nearby convenience stores I rotate between so that no one realizes just how much I drink. I start my daily binge at 5PM. — traditional time for happy hour, I rationalize — and drink my way into the wee hours of the morning.

Every night I get hammered to the point of blacking out, then crash on the couch. Sometimes I don't even make it to the couch and wake up in the middle of the living room floor. When I do, I try to ignore the numerous family photos around me, glaring down in judgment. I eventually rid the living room of the photos, stashing them in a dark corner of the walk-in closet in the bedroom.

One night at the 7-Eleven that's closest to me the clerk asks me point-blank, "Why do you drink?"

I'm flabbergasted. Ashamed. Angry. I have to think about it, and the answer I come up with is "Because it's fun." I cross that 7-Eleven off my rotation list and never go back.

River North is teeming with tony nightclubs, restaurants, and hotels — and, at night, drug dealers who cater to the tourists and hang out in front of the 7-Eleven on the corner of State and Hubbard. They're not hard to spot. They stand out from the packs of fancy-pants revelers migrating between the upscale establishments. Since I venture out every night, I begin to recognize faces — the same ones in the same spots, night after night. They might walk a block and then turn around and walk the block again, but they're always in the same general area. They're such neighborhood fixtures that their familiarity makes it seem as if I know them.

The first time I buy drugs, I do so on a whim. It happens one night when I venture out a little before 2AM, when liquor sales stop, with the intention of buying one more six-pack for the night. Innocent enough.

But then I spot a figure in front of the 7-Eleven where I'd planned to pick up my Blue Moons. He looks like a gangsta, but more put together and minus the chains. Shiny black bomber jacket, saggy jeans, impeccably clean, throwback red-and-black Air Jordans, White Sox baseball cap with a flat brim. Natty, shoulder-length dreads. If I had to guess, I'd say he's around twenty-three. He reminds me of Eazy-E from N.W.A. He smiles. Then he casts a nod my way. I nod back.

"Whatchu need?" And with those few words, my plans for the six-pack evaporate.

"Got any weed?" I ask, although I haven't touched the stuff in several years.

"Not today," he replies, "but I do have this." He opens up his fist to reveal a handful of little white rocks bundled up in plastic wrap. I don't even know what they are. "Best this side of town. I cooked it myself."

I don't even flinch when I see the crack. It seems like a good idea, the solution to breaking through the ceiling I'd been hitting in my quest to get even higher. There's just one problem.

"I don't have a pipe," I say.

He smiles. He knows he's landed a new customer. "Don't worry, come with me." He takes me to the alley behind State Street. I give him my twenty bucks, and after introducing himself as John he loads up his own pipe for me.

That first hit of crack. Goddammit! Holy fuck. It's like a punch in the gut — in a good way. An instantaneous head rush followed by a hypnotic numbness. It tastes like the smell of motorboat fuel emitted from an exhaust pipe on a hot summer day — unusual, but damn good. I'm already drunk, so it's hard to sort out my feelings. I feel the rush, and then … a vacuum.

Crack is supposed to be an upper; it's supposed to make you alert and euphoric. But for me, it's like a soft-core lullaby. Instead of the frenetic emotions of mania, I'm lulled into a cocoon of warmth and serenity that must be the closest feeling you can get to being back in the comfort and safety of the womb. I'm happy in my cocoon. Damn near blissful. But the euphoria lasts only ten minutes. You can see how it could become an expensive habit — fifty cents per minute. The desperate ones pay in nickels, dimes, and quarters they've solicited on the streets.

I go home and sleep like a koala. The next day I'm anxious for more. But getting fucked up is a night thing for me. My rationale: If I do it only at night, I'm not an addict.

Having gone to bed at 4AM the previous night, I get up at 4PM — which is convenient, because it means I have only an hour to kill before I can allow my bingeing to begin. I haven't showered or shaved in days. The dealers come out only at night, and it doesn't get dark until five-ish. When I'm high, the dark winter months don't bother me. I listlessly watch *Hardball* on MSNBC until darkness descends. Then I get my fix again.

John, laughing, observes my euphoria. "It feels good, right?"

"Hell yeah," I say.

And I'm loving it, riding the white pony to the end of the night.

* * *

A few days go by and I'm still getting to know the characters in my 'hood. I make friends with the dealers almost instantly. Everyone's very friendly and even professional, except for the dealer known as the Fat Girl. She specializes in heroin and occasionally has marijuana, but she rips me off one night, selling me a dimebag of bunk weed that she touts as "that LOUD shit" but, when I get home, turns out to be what I think is oregano. I should have known — they aren't pretty buds like normal — or at least smelled it. It's just shake, the fine flakes left over once all the good stuff has been picked through.

"That's not how we treat locals," John tells me, mumbling with a cigarette in his mouth. "If you're a tourist, that's another story, but regular customers, we give you quality product. Stick with me and I only give you the good shit."

I learn to trust no one except for John. John is my dealer and I can count on him — and only him — to get me high.

For me, crack is a social thing. I do it with John and the usual neighborhood suspects. I'm the only white guy. A dozen or so of us crackheads hang out on a loading dock and shoot the shit while sucking on the hot rock.

The alley becomes my Palace of Debauchery. Every night I'm not with my boyfriend, I come here after getting drunk on Miller High Life, having downgraded from my beloved Blue Moon so I can afford drugs. I smoke a rock or two and mellow out. I don't eat much, maybe a peanut butter and jelly sandwich if I'm not too lazy to buy bread and make one. In fact, if beer is the entrée, then crack is my digestif.

John smokes me up for free one night in the vestibule of an empty storefront on a quiet street. I don't know how many rocks we smoke, but it's the highest I've ever been in my life.

Pipe. Load. Rock. Fire. Inhale. Sizzle. Pupils. Dilated.

I'm climbing the stairway to heaven. Every night I get higher than the night before. It's time to up the ante, so I ask John about heroin. He pronounces it *hair-wawn*. "Sure, I can get you some *hair-wawn*," he says. "My boy from Englewood got it."

Imagine that. In River North, a neighborhood within striking distance of some of the most luxurious stores in the city — Prada, Burberry, Ferragamo — it's easier for me to score heroin than it is to find weed. No one ever has marijuana. Ever. It's all crack, powder cocaine, and heroin. For crystal meth, you gotta go up north to Boystown, the gayborhood of Chicago.

I've been curious about heroin ever since I learned my idol, Kurt Cobain, was an addict. I know you can buy hypodermic needles behind the counter at Walgreens. I'm tempted, but I'm afraid, so I don't cave. If shooting heroin is slam-dancing in a mosh pit of violent gutter punks, snorting is merely pogo-ing at a ska show. Snorting will do just fine.

Heroin's more expensive, so I don't share it with my pals at the Palace of Debauchery. I take it home. Heroin has a soothing effect on me. It's like going camping — you snuggle up in your sleeping bag and nestle by the fire as you enjoy a warm, empty place where calmness reigns. All that remains is tranquility. It wraps around you, shutting off your problems.

But that's the thing. It doesn't really shut off your problems. It exacerbates them. You become a vampire recluse. And you neglect everything, even things as simple as hygiene and laundry. If I had been negligent about looking for a job when I was just drinking, now the whole idea has gone out the window.

I smoke crack and do heroin for a couple months that winter, up until I go to rehab. Then I quit drinking and drugs altogether. I never get physically addicted to drugs — alcohol, yes, but not drugs. I never get busted. I'm never threatened with violence. I never spot a gun. I don't even witness any arguments, for that matter.

But I am slowly killing myself, spiraling downward without a tether to pull myself back into sober reality. And left to my own devices, I'd continue my downward spiral. But I'm one of the fortunate ones.

CHAPTER 2

A PICTURE-PERFECT CHILDHOOD

1979–1996

Watching me grow up, you would never guess that I would become a crack-smoking, alcoholic degenerate. My childhood is pure innocence, no traumas or incidents that might make a kid go off the rails. Sure, there are the usual childhood miseries, but I have a warm, supportive family and never experience anything worse than a run-in with a teacher or teasing from my peers. As for bipolar (still known as manic depression in my youth), that condition often doesn't emerge until people are older, often in their early thirties.

But a crack-smoking, alcoholic degenerate is what I've become, and my white-bread home is where the story begins.

I grow up in the very mainstream Lincoln Park on Chicago's North Side, a safe, middle-class neighborhood ideal for raising a family. My very first memory is of trying to breakdance to Michael Jackson's *Thriller* album. My four-year-old's moves are less than street worthy, and when my sister Colleen catches me gyrating on the shag carpeting of our townhouse basement, she probably mistakes my smooth moves for a seizure.

Most all of my childhood memories involve music in some form. Two years later, at Colleen's tenth-birthday party, my dad rents one or two new-fangled videotapes for her sleepover. I feel cool hanging out with the big kids. We watch *Flashdance* and *Footloose*. The dance sequences in both movies are like gymnastics or acrobatics and draw my attention more than any fight scene in *Star Wars*.

I'm the black sheep of the family music-wise — OK, *everything-wise*. My parents play stuff that doesn't resonate with me, such as Barry Manilow and Broadway cast albums. They don't own many records. Some kids learn about The Beatles or Led Zeppelin or even Simon & Garfunkel and Joni Mitchell from their parents. Not me. All of that is for me to discover on my own — and I'm fine with that, because I see music as something that belongs solely to me, even though it is my sister who introduces me to Madonna's *Like a Virgin*, The Police's *Synchronicity*, and The Go Go's' *Beauty and the Beat*. I love them all — and tracks such as "Material Girl," "Every Breath You Take," and "Our Lips Are Sealed" become the happy songs of my youth.

Unlike most kids, I have a stay-at-home dad — groundbreaking for the time. He's the one who bakes cupcakes for us, cooks dinner, takes us to swimming lessons, and cleans the house. My mom works long hours as a PR exec.

My childhood is filled with Cubs games at Wrigley Field and Bulls games at the peak of Michael Jordan's career. My whole family goes to street fairs to hear live music. Every year when the nearby Old Town Art Fair is held, Colleen and I set up an all-American lemonade stand and rake in the dough.

My family life is so wholesome that I'm not allowed to play with toy guns or even watch G.I. Joe cartoons, although my dad does make an allowance for a Super Soaker water pistol. Instead, Saturday mornings are spent with the polite, fresh-faced characters of *The Smurfs*, *Scooby Doo*, and *Muppet Babies*.

Then I enter Mrs. Feeney's first-grade class, and the illusion of my perfect childhood is shattered. Every day I am belittled or called out for typical six-year-old behavior — not putting the toys back, lagging behind on the way back from recess, or coloring outside the lines. Mrs. Feeney treats each of these misdeeds as misdemeanors, berating me in front of my peers. I begin to feel the first signs of what would later be diagnosed as generalized anxiety disorder.

One day, Mrs. Feeney makes fun of my Velcro sneakers, navy-and-green glow-in-the-dark Keds. "Look at those shoes. That's the wimpy way out. You don't wanna be a wimp, do you?" She glares, giving me a top-to-bottom glance. Her eyes are ice cold. "You should be tying your own shoes by now, Conor. You're not a baby anymore. Or are you? Earth to Conor: Velcro is for babies."

I take her attack on my fashion sense personally. I don't cry, but I tense up. I feel pain in my shoulders and my back.

Knocks like these happen on a daily basis.

Walking into her classroom is like stepping into a walk-in freezer. *Whooooosh!* All warmth and color is sucked out of the room.

My dad drives me to school, listening to NPR as usual. As we near St. Clement's, the opening theme for *Morning Edition* plays and I immediately feel like vomiting, because I know I am minutes away from entering that classroom. My dad has to drag me into the building protesting and whining every day. When my anxiety is particularly bad, I wet my pants on purpose so I can go home. Recognizing the situation is untenable, my parents opt to make a change.

I find myself sitting in the principal's office of my new public school. I'm looking down at the wood blocks of colored shapes littering the principal's desk. "Make a red rectangle, Conor," Mr. Anderson says. "Just take the blocks you see in front of you and pick the ones that will make the shape. Then shape it." Easy enough. Of course it is; this is a test for six-year-olds. I sit and stare into space.

"Conor, you can do it," my mom chimes in. But I sit stock-still. I can see exactly how to move the blocks to make the red rectangle, but anxiety has seized every fiber of my body. What if I make a mistake? What if I fail this simple test? I want to please my parents, but I'm frozen with the thought of letting them down.

Mr. Anderson moves on to the next test. "If you mix yellow and blue, what color do you get?" I just give a blank stare. The tension rises, even as the word "green" sits on the very tip of my tongue. I'm intimidated by authority figures. I refuse to take the test.

My parents want me to get into the accelerated program because the regular track at Lincoln Elementary has lower standards than my old one at St. Clement's. But because of my refusal to take the test, I'm relegated to the regular class. My fellow classmates are all impressed because I'm the only one who already knows how to read.

"Conor, it's time for morning story," Mrs. Edmonsen says each day. She lets me pick out a book and then read it to the class. My favorite is Maurice Sendak's *Where the Wild Things Are*. But I also read poetry from Shel Silverstein's *Where the Sidewalk Ends*.

Mrs. Edmonsen casts me in the lead of the school play, a biographical production about the early years of George Washington — chopping down the cherry tree, "I cannot tell a lie," and all that jazz. Underneath the house lights, I experience stage fright, but it's nothing like the anxiety I had in Mrs. Feeney's classroom. Once I hear the positive reaction from the audience, I swim through the rest of the play.

After that semester, I transfer to an all-boys private Catholic school, Hardey Prep. We wear uniforms: a clip-on tie (the wimpy way out again), navy-blue blazer with the red school insignia on the front pocket, and gray corduroys. The classes are much more challenging. I thrive in the new environment, where I dominate spelling bees and continue my burgeoning acting career, albeit in the wordless role of Astyanax in *The Trojan Women*, a production put on with the affiliated all-girls high school, Sacred Heart. It's an easy performance.

Even when I was only a tyke, my parents had pushed me into sports — basketball, soccer, you name it. I hate sports, but I play them anyway to please them. It doesn't matter how much I don't want to do something. If I'm asked, chances are I'll do it, especially for loved ones.

After I begin at Hardey, I start taking tennis lessons at the athletic club near our house. The only sport I like and am any good at is tennis, because I go to tennis camp every summer. I'm not competitive about it, I just like the simple action of hitting the ball back and forth. And that's most of what we do in camp — no drills, no suicide runs. It's just time spent outdoors, so I comply, even though I'd rather play Nintendo — NES role-playing games such as *Final Fantasy* and *Dragon Warrior*. I'm a proud geek.

Every summer, the family drives out to Six Flags Great America and rides the rickety wooden roller coaster, the American Eagle. I gaze in admiration at the older kids walking around the park in their metal T-shirts: Metallica, Megadeth, Slayer. At Six Flags, you wear your heavy-metal best.

It's the same at Milwaukee Summerfest, a music festival with numerous stages. One year we see Chubby Checker, which I enjoy just as much as my parents do, as well as R&B quartet and flavor-of-the-month Jodeci, Bon Jovi with Extreme, and my very first alternative-rock show, Stone Temple Pilots.

By the '90s, we've moved to a new house, still within the borders of Lincoln Park. The basement continues to serve as my own dance hall, although now I'm dancing to "It Takes Two" by Rob Base and DJ EZ Rock. It's my jam. The volume is cranked.

MTV's regular rotation is as white as fresh-fallen Chicago snow: Guns N' Roses, Aerosmith, and Poison. My friend Tyrone and I stay up all night watching *Video Soul* on BET and learning the latest dance moves. I'm enthralled by Janet Jackson as she struts through each track of *Rhythm Nation*.

Tyrone lives in Hyde Park, the mostly black neighborhood where the Obamas would live. We sneak watching *Madonna: Truth or Dare* in his basement one night when his older sister forgets to return the tape to the video store. It's a bit risqué for ten-year-old boys, but that's why we love it — that and the fact that the music is instantly iconic. We also play a hell of a lot of TurboGrafx 16, the video game system that's like an upscale Nintendo.

I love going to school dances, and Tyrone has been a good teacher. I dance the Running Man, the Roger Rabbit, and the Kid 'N' Play, a two-person routine with Tyrone. Everyone at the dances thinks I'm cool, and when I dance they surround me in a circle and chant, "Go Conor, go Conor!" With each step, another layer of my shyness falls away.

It's a boost of confidence that pulls me out of the dregs of the eighth-grade social hierarchy. Rather than getting belittled by my peers, I'm saluted. "You're kind of a nerd, but I like you because you can dance," one of the popular kids tell me one day. Even this half-assed compliment lifts my spirits. I'm not worthless after all.

On campus I may be a loser, but on the dance floor I'm king.

CHAPTER 3

PUNK ROCK
SAVED MY LIFE

1996–1998

Former bowling alley. West Side of Chicago. Sixteen lanes. Five-dollar admission. Beer-soaked carpet. Thick cigarette smoke. Butts stubbed out on the floor. Mohawks. Mosh pits. Skinheads. Silver-studded motorcycle jackets. The ceiling is nearly caving in and there's a tiny stage in the corner. Anarchy symbols are safety-pinned to black hoodies. Band patches too — prints on raggedy cloth: Bad Religion, Dead Kennedys, Sex Pistols, Black Flag, Minor Threat, The Exploited, The Misfits.

This is the Fireside Bowl, the punk mecca of Chicago. It's virtually the only place on the planet I feel at ease, where I feel like myself.

And it's not just because I'm surrounded by friends and other self-proclaimed freaks. The music itself is reason to come. During one of my early years at the Fireside, I catch Pittsburgh punks Anti-Flag. I scream along with gusto as they launch into their brand-spankin'-new political tirade: "You've gotta die, gotta die, gotta die for your government! Die for your country — that's shit!"

My social clique is an essential part of my support system. My green-mohawked friend Justin, who goes to public school and so doesn't have to worry about a dress code, is a sounding board for my newfound music-based politics. My hair is bleached. In fact, heads of hair bleached or dyed are everywhere at the Fireside. Cerulean blue. Royal purple. Fire-engine red. Fluorescent pink. The full spectrum of Crayola.

In high school, we punks are outcasts and nonconformists. The jocks and the cheerleaders torment us. We think they're boring and bland. It's a carefree time when we're at the Fireside, our hideaway from the hallways of horror that are high school.

Tonight, as Anti-Flag screams their anti-political screeds within the halls and alleyways of the Fireside, I find refuge from my first bout of depression, which has been set off by a series of seemingly small incidents that a younger, more resilient me would have easily brushed off.

The depression starts after I choose *Great Expectations* for a research paper on a major work of classic literature; I read three-quarters of the book and, after a fit of my usual procrastination, finish the rest via CliffsNotes. The paper comes back with a big red D and a note from Mr. Belmont: "A disappointing effort." I go into a funk. I obsess about it, replaying the words "disappointing effort" in my head over and over again. Usually when I write anything, even something I half-ass, I get an A.

Shortly after, Elisa, one of the top rankers in the school's social hierarchy, comes up to me in the hall and says, "Nobody likes you. You don't belong at this school. Everyone thinks you're a freak." I am a freak, but this comment still unsettles me, probably because I've felt that I haven't belonged since the moment I walked through the school's front door, and her words only reinforce my self-doubts.

I feel infinite anxiety and can't sleep that night. My palms sweat as I toss and turn, her words echoing, dominating my thoughts. For days I replay the scene in my head, my stomach roiling with discomfort. I'm beginning to hate high school more than your average bear, and I cannot break that feedback loop of Elisa's comments; it's a constant rumination, heavy as a boulder, a never-ending negativity directly pelting my soul. What's left of my ego is bludgeoned to near-death.

A few days later, Elisa says she doesn't believe the things she said about me and that she was just trying to give me a "complex." I'm not buying this sudden one-eighty. My ego remains on life support.

But at the Fireside, alongside the usual suspects, my spirits are lifted. It's as if every drumbeat pushes the depression farther away, while each cymbal crash kicks depression in the groin, and every power-chord drowns out the misery, making it less frightening, seemingly defeatable.

At the Fireside, there are no Elisas, only my fellow freaks. In addition to Justin, there's my girlfriend, Emily, whom I'm drawn to mostly because of her taste in music. (I've been struggling with my sexuality, but I've put that issue on the back burner while I deal with my other, more pressing stresses.) Emily is into ska, a horn-heavy music genre that's the precursor to reggae. Then there's Olivia, whom I met at a Sex Pistols concert and who spikes her naturally red hair with Elmer's Glue to ensure it stays up. Roxie Stardust — her nickname — comes from money and goes to the tony private school Francis Parker in Lincoln Park. My best friend Jack sports a safety pin piercing his ear and a shock of hair mussed with Vaseline to give him a decidedly Sid Vicious look. When we're not at the Fireside, we drive around the city in Roxie's black Ford Bronco, blasting Chicago punk like Screeching Weasel and Oblivion or classics like The Clash and The Ramones.

At the Metro, a larger venue, Olivia and Roxie pogo to a frantic NOFX song, fists pumping in the sea of raised arms. I don't do drugs. Punk is a natural high — the adrenaline that fuels my teenage years.

Roxie's parents go out of town frequently, but we rarely use the occasion to drink or do drugs. The kids in the suburbs throw keggers. We find our own fun. Sometimes we have weed. When we do, we go and sit on the rocks along Lake Michigan and smoke up. It's a nice environs for the occasional smoke-out. I'm not exactly straightedge, shunning all recreational substances, but I subscribe to enough straightedge tenets to use that as an excuse not to indulge. My friends respect my decision.

When Slapstick headlines at the Fireside during my junior year, we skank to the ska-punk beat. Offbeat strums of an electric guitar mingle with blaring trombones and trumpets and the scratchy voice of the band's leader, Brendan Kelly. The frequent bursts of distorted guitar echo during the choruses.

The show is sold out, with people standing in the bowling alleys, but my friends and I are lucky. We've come early enough to get inside, away from the February chill.

I'm a social butterfly at the Fireside. Socializing is usually not my strong suit, but here I'm popular because I know so much about the music. The Fireside keeps me sane, makes me feel I'm part of a community of like-minded souls. Sometimes, after a night chatting up the crowd, I feel confident enough to approach the band after the show.

"I really dig your album. It's equal parts Operation Ivy and Less Than Jake," I say to Brendan, the band's frontman and current singer for The Lawrence Arms.

"Fuck yeah! Those are two of my favorite bands. We're playing at the VFW Hall in Elgin next weekend," he says. "You should come. Keep coming back."

"Keep coming back" — these three words I would hear later, chanted after the Serenity Prayer at the end of every AA meeting. Indeed, being at the Fireside is like a mass catharsis we get nowhere else in our lives. It's a fellowship.

I plaster my bedroom walls with neon pink and orange flyers from various punk shows of local bands: Slapstick. Alkaline Trio.

31

Naked Raygun. No Empathy. Chicago's burgeoning scene may not rival those of California or New York, but it comes close.

Punk is a rush, an instant tingling all over. It's worlds away from the feeling I get when I go to school, where I'm an outcast. I'm a good student, but the few friends I have are of the fair-weather variety, kids I have no social interactions without outside of eating lunch. I forget them the moment the bell rings, but I carry thoughts of my Fireside friends all day long. I wonder what class they're in, what they're eating for lunch, if they are as alone at their schools as I am at mine.

It's not long before I abandon my straightedge status and try marijuana for the first time. Emily always has weed. She carries it with her everywhere, caching it in a dimebag inside a metal Altoids box padded with potpourri to disguise the smell. She smokes all the time with her South Side friends, but not around me. She knows I'm a pot virgin.

For many of us alcoholics, that first sip of alcohol is like bathing in sunlight on a tropical island. Warm and pure. Hypnotic and eye opening. Just plain wonderful.

My first drunken experience comes comparatively late in the game, during senior year of high school on a college visit to St. Louis University. Thom, a SLU sophomore, is assigned to show me the ropes, so I stay in his dorm, where he introduces me to the wonders of "Natty Light," as college students refer to Natural Light beer.

I'm hooked as soon as I realize that beer demolishes my shyness and turns me into a confident, outgoing person. I practically glow.

At the Fireside, in my comfort zone, I can be gregarious, but in life outside of punk rock, I am still as shy as it gets. Thom brings me to a house party where I talk with everyone, laugh at every joke.

"What's the difference between a punk and a metalhead?" someone posits. "The metalheads can actually play their instruments."

A drunk me thinks it's the funniest joke I've ever heard.

But one night I decide I want to try pot, so we and her friends smoke up in a bank parking lot on the South Side of Chicago. It gives me a roasty-toasty feeling, a tingling all over. Many people don't get high the first time, but I do. I bum a Marlboro from one of Emily's friends. It's my first cigarette, and it enhances the experience of that high. My heart beats even more intensely.

The next day, I call Jack to tell him about my first time getting stoned. "It was magical," I tell him, just as I hear the call-waiting beep. "You gotta come with us next time." I click over to the other line. It's my dad. After a brief conversation, I click back, not realizing it's now become a three-way call. My dad overhears everything. He gets home and yells at me. The mild-mannered dad I've always known and loved is nowhere to be seen. He screams so loud that I can almost visualize him onstage at the Fireside. But I'm snapped out of my reverie when he announces that I'm grounded for a month.

I feel I've let my parents down. I'm not full-blown depressed, but guilt pools in the pit of my stomach. Strangely, it's the same kind of guilt I feel on my birthdays, like I don't deserve so much love, even if it's tough love. Birthdays have always been sad moments for me.

But being grounded doesn't curtail my experimenting. At first, marijuana mellows me out, smoothing my usual nervous energy. It masks my depression, which has swelled to physical, painful levels. My brain hurts, today and every day. I've called myself depressed before, but it's really been just a bigger sadness, a slow motion that drags me through the day.

Marijuana helps me deal with things like Elisa's tirade. But then the mean weed shows its true colors. I get paranoid and consumed with anxiety. I can't even leave the house stoned, or I'll panic. For that reason, much as I've enjoyed my first pot experience, I smoke only a handful of times in high school.

Looking back on my punk-rock years, I realize what a special time this was. The Fireside Bowl saved me from the evils of the preppy hostiles out to get me at St. Ignatius. It was my sanctuary.

In a show of unity, the whole crew — Olivia, Jack, Justin, Emily — and I speed along Chicago's picturesque lakefront in Roxie's ride, blasting the 1977 debut album by The Clash. We sing "Complete Control" in unison, screaming, "I don't judge you. Why do you judge me?" — which are, in fact, not the correct lyrics. It's our "Bohemian Rhapsody"–*Wayne's World* moment. But it means more than that because of the message.

That is what the punk scene gives us: unconditional acceptance of who we are and what we stand for. Respect. We are bound by our own simple punk ideal that weird is cool. It doesn't matter that we get the lyrics wrong. The sentiment is enough.

We're biding our time in high school, knowing that salvation lies just on the other side of graduation. In the meantime, we abide by our punk ethos: To be rebellious. To be angry. To be cool in our own, unique way. To laugh. To scream. To be a misfit.

Punk helps me realize that I can make it through high school. I may still be a freak when I get to college, but there's bound to be more like me. I'll fit right in.

CHAPTER 4

IDIOTS OUT WANDERING AROUND

1997

Iowa State University is in the middle of nowhere in Ames, a half-hour drive from the state capital of Des Moines. There are cows grazing across the street from my freshman dorm. And combines, too, although I'm not exactly sure what a combine is.

Having grown up in a big city, I opt to attend a university in the sticks so I can study without distraction. The fact that my mom is an Iowa State alum and that the campus — designed by Frederick Law Olmstead, the landscape architect responsible for Central Park — is idyllically scenic are added draws. In my first year, I form a close-knit circle of friends with other liberally minded former urbanites. We find comfort in having found each other in such a conservative setting.

In my dorm room one night, we sit around watching *The Wizard of Oz* set to the music of Pink Floyd's *Dark Side of the Moon*. Urban legend has it that if you press play on the third roar of the Metro-Goldwyn-Mayer lion, the lyrics match what's happening in the film. As I smoke my clove cigarette, I realize the legend is just a myth perpetuated by stoners. But it's fun anyway.

This is the night my binge-drinking starts.

I'm swilling Boone's Farm wine, which costs $2.79 a bottle and comes in flavors like Tickle Pink and Sun Peak Peach. It's nasty but it's what my college budget can afford, and my friends and I don't smoke weed because we can never get it. If we were part of the Greek system, we'd have no trouble. But among us dorm rats, no one has it.

There's a lot of sugar in Boone's Farm wine. It's cloyingly sweet, and I end up getting sick after finishing the bottle. The upchuck starts somewhere around the first appearance of the flying monkeys. I vomit in the hallway.

Although drinking excessively is not uncommon in college, I start going at it on a fairly regular basis, managing to confine the bingeing to Thursday through Sunday. I can never have just a few drinks, so whenever I'm around alcohol, I end up bingeing. I'm the ringleader on our corridor, always the one to initiate a drink-fest. Fred, a junior, buys for us, as long as we return the favor and pick him up a pack of smokes. It's a symbiotic relationship.

Yet I am a good student. I study magazine journalism and work at both the campus newspaper, *The Iowa State Daily*, and *Ethos*, the school magazine. I'm also a DJ at KURE, the college radio station.

My roommate, Colin, is a conservative fundamentalist Christian. In high school, he had to hide his contraband U2 CDs from his parents, who only allowed him to listen to Christian bands like Jars of Clay and Audio Adrenaline.

I take him on as my project: Project Colin Corruption. I do this partly for fun, but mostly so I can have a drinking partner. I expose Colin to all kinds of secular music, the angrier the better. I imagine how horrified his mom would be to walk in on him listening to Ministry, KMFDM, or anti-establishment punk. The thought makes me smile.

At first Colin is reticent about drinking. But of course drinking is ubiquitous in college. He can't hide forever.

One night we get Fred to buy us a bottle of peach schnapps so we can make fuzzy navels, which I choose because the candy-like taste makes them seem less objectionable than, say, doing shots of tequila. After hesitating, Colin finally takes a sip of his fuzzy navel. He beams like he just found heaven and proceeds to down a series of them almost faster than I can mix them. Two hours later, he's retching in the dorm bathroom.

Soon enough we graduate to mixing orange juice with not peach schnapps but Everclear — grain alcohol that is 190 proof (more than twice the alcohol content of standard-issue vodka).

By November, Colin is drinking on a regular basis and has even picked up a clove cigarette habit, to the point where I have to ask him not to smoke in front of my computer so as not to damage the hardware. Despite my chastising, I'm proud of my protégé. Mission accomplished.

My best friend in college is Shar, a Filipino-American from the suburbs of Chicago who bucks the stereotype about engineers. Rather than being a shy, conservatively dressed introvert, she's the hippest, most outgoing person on campus. She really digs music and also works at the radio station.

Our circle of friends includes graphic designers, the gay crowd, people who work at KURE and the *Daily*, English geeks, architecture students, mathematicians and physicists, and philosophy majors. Shar, the outlier engineer, would be a perfect fit with the old Fireside gang.

At KURE, you can pass on your shift if you need to study, have an exam, or are leaving early for Christmas break. During finals week, Shar volunteers to work a twenty-four-hour "suicide shift."

As much as I love music, the mere thought of having to come up with programming for a full twenty-four hours causes me anxiety. Decision-making is not my strong suit, which is one of the reasons I'm such a procrastinator. Even picking what to play next is difficult for me. Sometimes I write out lists when I DJ.

But Shar's got it all planned out. She doesn't write out a list. The CDs at the station are all in alphabetical order. She's gonna play the alphabet — not the ABCs, but the QWERTY keyboard. From Queen to My Bloody Valentine. Shar takes the opportunity to the extreme, and I'm in awe.

Shar invites her single friends to an I Hate Valentine's Day party, where we bleach each other's hair and then dye it pink or green or blue. I already have blue-and-red devil horns that stick up in front of my closely shaved head.

One of the most important things I've learned so far at college is that drinking the sweet stuff induces vomiting, so I've grown into a beer drinker. Beer is my drink of choice, even though it's shitty beer like Budweiser or Miller Lite.

But we never go to keggers. Keggers are for frat boys and sorority girls. We make our own fun. That's what happens when you live in a town of just over 47,000.

At one party, a guy named Sten is debating the origins of the Pythagorean Theorem. I'm talking with Pinto, who's taken his nickname from *Animal House*, about the musical prowess of the Pixies and their influence on Nirvana. The consensus is that "Smells Like Teen Spirit" is in fact kind of a Pixies ripoff, just as Nirvana bassist Krist Noveselic has admitted.

As I glance around at my ragtag but utterly lovable group of friends, I feel like we've created our own Fireside, right here amid the cornfields of Ames, Iowa.

When I'm not with my friends, I spend most of my college time at *The Daily*, where I become arts and entertainment editor, a job that comes with the perks of free CDs and concert tickets. At the Maintenance Shop, the café-cum-music-venue in the student union, I can just walk right in without a ticket. With Shar and my other friends, I see bands like Japanese indie-pop duo Cibo Matto, British punkers the Buzzcocks, third-wave ska group the Scofflaws, and Digital Underground, the hip-hop group best known for "The Humpty Dance."

Even when a concert lands on a designated binge night, I manage to stay sober. I don't yet have a fake ID anyway. My

41

appetite for alcohol is as strong as your grandpappy's moonshine, so sometimes I wish I had thought to bring a flask of Everclear. But I've never really enjoyed straight-up hard liquor, and besides, it's good to be sharp as a tack when I'm reviewing these shows. I take notes throughout.

Sophomore year I move to a new dorm and room with Alastair, a Scottish exchange student from the University of Glasgow who's studying sports physical therapy. His accent is as thick as the smoke at the Fireside. On day one of our roommate-hood, we go to Wal-Mart. I get a kick out of the fact that Alastair calls shopping carts trolleys.

We room together for only a semester before I go off to Europe to study in Madrid through St. Louis University. Although I'm thrilled to be out of the cowtown, I mostly keep to myself because I can't identify with the majority of the students who, just as in high school, are preppy and there to party, not to learn.

I live with Pilar, an older woman in her sixties who takes in students and lives right around the corner from the Royal Palace. She cooks extravagant homemade meals for us — everything from paella to *flamenquín,* a sort of breaded stick made from rolled ham and pork — and even does our laundry. I hang out with a lot of locals even though my Spanish isn't the greatest. I can understand a lot more than I can say. We go to discotheques and dance to electronic music, pop, salsa (I take lessons), or rock.

Whenever I go out on the weekends, Pilar pulls me aside and says, *"Cone-nor, no bebas"* —"Conor, don't drink." She knows. I'm a heavy drinker even by Spanish standards.

One Saturday night I find myself alone and drink an entire half-pint of Jack Daniels in the Plaza España, then barf in the bathroom when I get home. I'm not used to straight-no-chaser. Pilar is not happy.

Spring break, during Semana Santa (Holy Week), my high school friend and fellow punker Olivia comes to visit. We go down south to Granada to watch the street processions, where the local brotherhoods re-create the Passion of the Christ and parade down the streets.

I've booked a room, but the hotel has lost our reservation, leaving us homeless for the night. As we wander the streets, we end up making friends with Carlos and his three droogs from Madrid, who are in the same boat as us but with a broken-down car being fixed in a garage. Recognizing there's safety in numbers, our two groups decide to band together and set up camp in a park.

We smoke hash, drink sangria from huge juice boxes, and spend most of the night getting high and drunk. Our newfound friends teach us a small dictionary's worth of Spanish slang and dirty words. "*La leche*" (the milk) is like the English equivalent of calling something "the bomb." When something's awesome, it's "*de puta madre*" (literally "the mother slut" or "the mother fuck"), while something that's total shit is "*la puta mierda*." After a couple more hours of smoking, I feel practically fluent.

Hashish is really rare in the States. I love it and hope I can score some whenever I get back home. It feels the way marijuana does for other people — calming. And it tastes delicious: subtly sugary, like cannabis-flavored cotton candy.

We chat in Spanish interspersed with some English throughout the night, discussing politics and pop-culture — everything from the Monica Lewinsky scandal to the anarchist movement in Madrid. When fatigue begins to wear us down, we head to a nearby Dumpster, where we find cardboard boxes and bubble wrap to serve as a softer foundation to sleep on.

The next morning I wake up shivering and see the sun rise over the Sierra Nevada. It's a unique night — my favorite night in Europe, actually. Who knew urban camping could be so much fun?

When the semester ends, I spend three weeks traveling on my own to Europe's greatest hits: Paris, Rome, Florence, Berlin, London, Dublin, and onward. Being alone, I'm a magnet for meeting other people, and I make friends with fellow travelers from all over the world. I tell myself that one day I'll live in Europe.

By the time I reach my junior year, I'm so involved with activities I don't have time to feel depressed. I'm practically working full-time at *The Daily*, contributing to the school magazine, and maintaining my weekly two-hour show at the radio station, all while balancing schoolwork. I'm also living on a Spanish-speaking dorm floor.

Rave culture hits Iowa around 1999 or so. Iowa is late to the game, but not impervious. I go to a rave called Crop Circles in a cornfield outside Ankeny, where DJs spin everything from trance to acid house for partiers who have come from as far away as Chicago, Minneapolis, and Kansas City. Green lasers and the headlights of a circling tractor illuminate the space. Smoke machines add to the ambience. I start interviewing people — the promoter, DJs — for a cover story for *Ethos*. I'm technically working, so I don't do ecstasy, but it's around. I regret never doing it.

A handful of friends are renting a big off-campus house they've dubbed the Jiggle-o-drome. Or is it Gigolo-drome? Either way, they throw frequent parties. One night I find myself with Catherine, a woman who has a huge crush on me, sitting on my lap. Since we live in the same dorm, after the party we walk home together and share a drunken kiss in the elevator. I'm still in denial, trying to make heterosexuality work, and the kiss doesn't feel right. At least when I'd kiss or even fool around with Emily, there'd been a sense of novelty to it. With Catherine, it's just all wrong. But we continue seeing each other despite never taking it to the next level. I know it's selfish, but she's my beard. I convince myself that I'm not gay, that I have a "girlfriend."

When Shar asks what the deal is between me and Catherine, I shrug it off, saying we're just friends. "Dude, you're totally leading her on. That's not cool," she chides.

Shar probably already knows I'm gay, even if I'm not ready to admit it to myself. I know she hangs with several gay guys and is a straight "ally" in the campus LGBT Alliance. College is more than half over, and I still don't have it figured out.

* * *

That summer I land my dream internship at *Rolling Stone* magazine in New York. I live on 14th Street in the NYU dorms. I never get to write anything, but I feel honored to have been chosen over the slew of other applicants. I'm assigned minor tasks like getting coffee and sorting through the mail, much of which comes from prisoners, which I think is pretty cool. Every morning I get the managing editor's breakfast: a buttered poppy-seed roll and a large black coffee. One day I am happily tasked with fetching a bottle of water for Slash, the guitarist from Guns N' Roses. I immediately fall in love with New York and decide to move there after college.

Senior year, Shar and I get a three-bedroom apartment together near Campustown, where all the bars and restaurants are. Gordon, an English major, moves in with us too. She gets a pet rat, Mabel, named after a song by LA ska-punk band Goldfinger.

This is when I finally realize that in fact I am gay all day. Gordon is, for some reason, on the mailing list for the *International Male* catalog, a PG-13 glossy with beefcake gents in tighty-whities. It's like a first taste of pornography for me. So now I know. I'm too nervous to act on it and, I tell myself, because I'm too busy for a relationship. But I *know*.

For spring break, while most of the other students go off to Cancun or Panama Beach, Shar and I visit Alastair in Scotland. He drives us around the countryside, but we can barely walk past the side of the road because it's taped off. Foot-and-mouth disease is gripping the country. No hiking for us.

Alastair shows us around Glasgow, where he goes to "Uni." I find the city cosmopolitan and edgy. We go to a dance club and have a blast. We play snooker at a pub. Then Alastair takes us up north to his hometown of Kirriemuir, in the northern part of Scotland. Population 5,910. There's a Peter Pan statue in the town square to commemorate the birthplace of playwright J. M. Barrie, who wrote the original story.

Kirriemuir has one pub, where I get drunk on Tennent's Scottish Lager. I'm always drinking a bit faster than my friends, and I'm good and sloshed by the time I flop into bed at Alastair's childhood home. Still drunk, I get up in the middle of the night in search of the bathroom and stumble into his mom's bedroom. I remain in the doorway for a moment, unsure what to do or if I've woken her. Then, as softly as I can, I close the door behind me and tiptoe back to bed, forgetting I have to pee.

She cooks us a bountiful breakfast the next morning. There is haggis involved, but she says we don't have to try it if we don't want to. I don't know if I can handle sheep stomach with a hangover.

September of my senior year, I finally turn twenty-one. Shar, Gordon, and I go bar hopping and end up at the Lost and Found, where it's $1.25 rum-and-Coke night. I go way overboard and end up vomiting in the dirty bathroom. The vomit is black from the Coke.

Drink specials are out of control at Iowa State. There's 75-cent gin-and-tonic night at Thumbs, a townie bar around the corner from our apartment. There's also $1.25 strawberry daiquiri night at Welch Ave. Station. Beer is super-cheap too. We follow all the drink specials and become such frequent patrons that I soon memorize the specials for each night. Now we can drink *every* night!

When I graduate that spring, I look back at my college experience and am glad I didn't go to NYU, UCLA, or some other big-city school. I'd wanted something different, to be outside my comfort zone. Back in Chicago, I'd never even come into contact with Republicans, but in Ames, it was impossible to avoid them, even if I'd wanted. Iowa State forced me to think about politics from a different perspective. I was a minority — just like when I was punk in high school.

In college, we'd made our own fun. Whether it was a pajama party or a dead-rock-star party or even just chilling in the sunshine on the quad, we were happy to be in Iowa. Where else could I have DJ'd as a piddly freshman, been a top editor at the newspaper sophomore year, lived with a small-town Scotsman, drank 75-cent gin and tonics, and gone to a rave in a cornfield? I'd chosen wisely, even if my liver didn't concur.

After a short visit with my parents in Chicago, I land a writing job at AOL. We pack up the Saturn and my dad drives me to New York. Three weeks later, 9/11 happens.

CHAPTER 5

I LOVE NEW YORK

2001

It's an absolute knockout day. Sun is shining, temperature is warm. I'm in such a good mood I practically skip onto the F train, which is elevated throughout most of Brooklyn. But today the view is devastating.

I see the towers smoking. Everyone on the train is freaking out. The train goes underground to cross under the East River into Manhattan. The entire car buzzes with conjecture. Everyone is pensive but not yet frightened. Is this a planned demolition we haven't heard about? After all, some New Yorkers consider the Twin Towers to be an eyesore.

When I emerge from the subway at 14th Street, the first tower is down. An avalanche of white smoke and dust drenches lower

Manhattan. As I stand on Sixth Avenue watching the smoking wreckage, I see the second tower go down.

I haven't yet learned about the planes. I'm such an eternal optimist and so giddy about being in New York, terrorism doesn't even cross my mind. As I'm standing on Sixth Avenue watching the second tower fall, there are small gasps of awe around me. Apparently everyone else is as oblivious as I am about what's happening and thinks this is like some Las Vegas casino demolition, which means the buildings would have been evacuated.

I'm late for work as I ride the elevator up to the eighth floor of our Chelsea office building, more than a mile north of the towers. When the door opens, I see my boss and several coworkers.

"Go home, it's an attack!" my boss says with urgency as she steps onto the elevator with me. I don't listen, partly because this is the first time I've heard this news and I don't fully believe it, and partly because I know what I have to do. I get off the elevator and decide to call my parents on a landline because I know cell reception will be jammed. I'm lucky to get through.

"Oh my God! Conor! Are you OK?" My mom answers on the first ring. I assure both parents that I'm fine, then spend the rest of the day watching CNN in horror before heading home to my apartment in Windsor Terrace, Brooklyn.

The next day I walk around Union Square, where the usual breakdancers have ceded their space to a makeshift memorial. I see flowers and candles everywhere, as well as bulletin boards with flyers bearing pictures of people with messages asking "Have you seen this person?" I cry.

It turns out I know one of the slain. Vanessa Kolpak. I went to high school with her and think she was on student council, and she was working in the financial industry in one of the towers. I didn't know her very well, but it makes the tragedy personal.

I begin drinking more than usual, mostly at home with my roommate, Andy. We avoid the topic of 9/11, and our unspoken thoughts hang as heavy in the air as the alcohol fumes.

Somehow, my depression remains manageable, probably because for once I'm not alone in my depression. I have millions of other New Yorkers to be depressed with, and that somehow makes it OK.

In the weeks after 9/11, a pall of stunned solemnity hangs over the city, like some sci-fi mist that has zapped us of any ray of cheer. No one who works in an office does anything for the first couple of weeks, so I spend my days watching CNN and my nights drowning my sorrows in Rolling Rock, my current beer of choice.

I've never hung out in the Financial District — it's mostly office buildings and bars and restaurants that cater to the Wall Street folks. Now it's a scar on the stoic face of the self-proclaimed capital of the world.

The city, a place renowned for its bustle and fast-paced lifestyle, is on mute. And pause. No one's selling weed in Washington Square Park. There are no street performers. On the contrary, it's a wasteland. I've never seen Times Square so empty. No tourists. No people going to work. The few I meet on the street speak quietly and walk slowly; 9/11 has us stumbling blind through the urban jungle without purpose. I feel like I'm exploring a New York in a different time-space continuum.

We return to work two weeks later. I enjoy my job at AOL, where I pass my time editing city pages for Albany and Buffalo, New York. Plus, my coworkers are also twentysomethings, so we all go out for drinks many nights. It doesn't matter that I come to work hungover, because the job is so undemanding.

After 9/11, I feel as if the world could end at any moment. It's the impetus for me to finally do something about the fact that I'm gay. What's the worst that could happen? The world's going to end anyway.

On a lark, I kiss a guy for the first time at Wonder Bar in the East Village. The guy just happens to be my roommate, Andy. He becomes my first boyfriend.

* * *

New York is crazy, which means I fit in perfectly. People are weird in a good way. It's as if all the freaks from high school moved here and were anointed the cool kids. Statuses are reversed. Freaky is cool. The jocks can suck it. In fact, the freakier the better in this town. We own the city.

Within the city's borders, Williamsburg in Brooklyn is the freak epicenter, its star on the rise as the hipster capital of the world. Formerly an enclave for Hassidic Jews, the neighborhood is just beginning its gentrification, which means our options are limited to a record store or two, a handful of cool bars and restaurants, a live-music venue, and art galleries-cum-nightclubs. In these early days of Williamsburg 2.0, you might find a bona fide starving artist selling his paintings on the street. In fact, everyone who lives in the neighborhood is a musician, poet, fashion designer, photographer — anything on the creative spectrum.

The Bedford Avenue L train station, located on Williamsburg's main drag, is just one stop from Manhattan. That's why all the hipsters are moving here — because it's cheap (compared with Manhattan proper) and easily accessible to the East Village and Lower East Side, which still out-hip Williamsburg. Stickers, flyers, and roommate ads blanket every surface of every street pole and abandoned storefront, giving the neighborhood an aura of an outdoor CBGB.

The unofficial Bedford Avenue fashion parade has no peer: hipsters dressed to the nines in their thrift-store best — and again, the weirder, the better; rail-thin guys in girl jeans; tight vintage T-shirts that seem to come from a tween brother's wardrobe; women in granny dresses or legwarmers straight out of an aerobics class circa 1984.

It feels like I'm living an "I was there" moment. Like Greenwich Village in the '60s or Paris in the '20s. I lap up the bohemian culture.

Andy and I are regulars at a party called Berliniamsburg, a mix of gay and straight held at a venue called Luxx. We dance next to women with asymmetrical haircuts to match their asymmetrical tops. Trannies and drag queens contribute to the festive atmosphere. Sexy guys, gay and straight, fill the rest of the space. And I always, always arrive drunk before I hit the dance floor, especially since we only get there at 1 or 2AM. Even though there's plenty of coke to go around, I prefer to get high on alcohol.

I experience my first bout of hypomania on that dance floor. I'm busting a move to Fischerspooner's one and only hit, "Emerge." Everyone is dancing as if we're on the verge of atomic war and this is our last night out on Earth. Dance floor ... on ... fire! A shirtless dude in tight leather pants and a pink feather boa casts a gaze my way. He resembles a young Iggy Pop amid a crowd already echoing David Bowie–era glam, and I imagine that I'm indeed partying with the legendary music icons. In my hypomanic mind I'm at Studio 54, famous enough to get past the velvet rope and party like a rock star with rock stars. Maybe I'm a top editor at *Rolling Stone.* I've heard that doing cocaine makes you feel on top of the world; but I'm not just on top. I *own* it. The alcohol fuels my mania, so that I'm practically soaring above the dance floor, looking down on everyone else as I rule from on high. I think how cool my life is and wonder what my family would think if they could see me. Would they think I was a weirdo? Hell, yeah. I'm one proud weirdo.

Berliniamsburg is supposed to be like going to a Berlin disco-theque back in the '80s. DJ Larry Tee, the mastermind of the movement that would become a short-lived festival, spins a new style of music called electroclash. His roster of artists — Avenue D, W.I.T., Jonny McGovern (a.k.a., the Gay Pimp) — are still just blips on the NYC music radar. The grinding, grimy keyboard flourishes provide the backbone of this music. There are electronic handclaps. Distorted vocals. Flares of rapid-fire machine-gun beats. The music is acidic and gnarly. Beeps and bleeps lie underneath what sound like synthesized lightsabers and ray guns. Filthy lyrics to boot.

Berliniamsburg is now legendary in the pantheon of New York City nightlife. But electroclash never really catches on beyond Brooklyn — maybe a little bit in London — or if it does, it's limited to a few artists like Fischerspooner, Peaches, and ADULT. Luxx becomes my new Fireside. We feel we're part of something special, an exclusive underground electronic dance scene.

My AOL friends and I create a second home at Motherfucker, a party that bounces around to different venues each holiday weekend. We always pre-party at Julie's shoebox of a studio in the East Village, slamming back drinks while perched on a ragtag collection of chairs and even the bathtub, which is in the kitchen. I can outdrink most anyone, at nearly twice their rate. By the time we leave, we're all sloshed, but I'm definitely in the lead.

Sometimes Motherfucker is held at the legendary Roxy night-club in Chelsea, where a sea of some 6,000 people pack themselves in as tightly as pills in a freshly filled prescription. Ecstasy is for sale on the dance floor. DJ Michael T, who isn't a household name but is New York famous, hosts the party, spinning a variety of '80s new wave, goth, industrial, late-era disco, and electronic.

I like to take in the eye candy from the skybox-like balcony, from where I can spot many a hot shirtless gay guy. This is the sort of party where even straight guys might wear black lipstick, as if channeling Tim Curry in *The Rocky Horror Picture Show*. That's the style. Motherfucker incarnate.

I'm not a club kid like James St. James or Richie Rich, but I do go out almost every night. Drunk-kissing Andy on the dance floor is a regular occurrence.

I finally tell my sister I'm gay when I come home for Thanksgiving. She actually already has me figured out. She pressures me to tell my parents, which I do on a trip to Chicago on St. Patrick's Day weekend.

"Can we sit down and have a chat?" I say.

"Sure," my mom responds.

I'm about to do it. I'm about to come out as gay to my parents. I'm stuck in the mud with anxiety. I have sweaty palms, an anxiety symptom that only grows worse later on in my life. I imagine that my mom will be fine with my announcement and that my dad will be weirded out. It's tough to find the words, even though I've already written them down and practiced. But after a deep breath, I let it out.

"You know I love the St. Patrick's Day parade in Chicago," I say, starting off slowly. "But there's actually another reason for my trip. I have something to tell you ... and what I want to tell you is that I'm gay."

Dead silence for twenty seconds. Then my mom starts to cry. "Are you gonna get AIDS now?" she blurts.

Surprisingly, my dad is cool with it. He just says "OK," nothing more. I remember watching a *60 Minutes* report about gay people with him when I was a teenager and he turned to me and said,

"Well, we're lucky we don't have any of *that* in our family." I guess that, like Obama, my dad has evolved on his position.

That night, my dad takes me to see the Chicago Symphony Orchestra. It's soothing, the perfect medicine to get my mind off things. It would be awkward if my mom took me, but because my dad has been somewhat supportive, I feel comfortable. A couple of months later, my mom finally comes to terms. It's all good. No tension anymore.

My dream job falls into my lap when my friend Nate from the college newspaper hooks me up. I start working for MTV News as a researcher and fact checker. I have never done TV before. The writing is different: short and to the point. The scripts are in ALL CAPS. Every word counts. A couple of years later I become a producer, writing scripts for three- to five-minute spots.

Over the course of my time at MTV, I am lucky to interview the Beastie Boys, Green Day, and Chuck D of Public Enemy, among others. I get to cover events like Lollapalooza, South by Southwest, and the Grammy Awards. I also do more serious fare, such as going to Littleton, Colorado, to interview high school students and write about the fifth anniversary of Columbine. Another serious piece I write is a primer on the crisis in Darfur. It's an intellectually stimulating job.

And I love it, while it lasts.

CHAPTER 6

THE HIGH LIFE

2004–2007

I've just cut a wrap-up piece on the Grammys and am out to celebrate. I'm seated in a banquette at Blue Ribbon, one of the finest restaurants in Brooklyn, eating oysters and drinking champagne on my first date with Chris, whom I've met on gay.com.

The place is sprawling with fancy tables and chairs, the kind you might find at a bistro in Paris. Mood lighting illuminates the space. Everyone is dressed up, but we're wearing T-shirts.

"How did you get into playing music?" I ask.

"I grew up in Indiana and there was nothing else to do," he says, downing a Blue Point oyster. The mignonette you spoon over the Long Island crustaceans is fresh and vibrant. The shallots really stand out. "Life revolves around church in that corner of the world, and I wasn't interested. I wanted to emulate my favorite rock stars."

"I'm not religious either," I say, as the waiter returns to refill our champagne flutes, the bottle on ice between us. "I play guitar too, but not nearly as well as you, I'm sure." I've already learned during our email exchanges that he's a talented musician who studied at Boston's Berklee College of Music, renowned as the best of its kind in the country. He writes theme songs for television as well as sports shows like *NHL on Fox* and NASCAR. He can play Guns N' Roses' entire *Appetite for Destruction* note for note, including guitar solos. And he's got a sparkly gold Gibson guitar, just like Slash. I'm impressed.

We have the standard back-and-forth first-date chat. Get us started on rock 'n' roll and we can't stop talking. He's wearing a Rolling Stones T-shirt, with the big red tongue. We ponder the age-old question of Beatles vs. Stones. I'm a Beatles guy. He's a Stones guy. Maybe opposites do attract.

There are no pauses in the conversation. I order the braised beef shoulder and he gets the steamed lobster. It's all more expensive than I can afford, but he insists on paying. Most dates I go on involve one drink at a bar, but not this one: it's three courses plus dessert.

He's the first guy I've been on a date with since breaking up with my second boyfriend and being single for a while. It's clear from the start we aren't looking for hookups. We click almost instantly, mostly because of our mutual obsession with music.

The date is going swimmingly, and we head back to his Park Slope apartment, where he serenades me with an improvised jazz-guitar jam. Then he sings "Jane Says," by Jane's Addiction. It's not hard to win me over with a gesture like that. I break my rule and we have sex on the first date. We spend the night together and have breakfast in the morning. As we wake up, the smell of stale alcohol is on his breath and I realize mine probably smells the same. But neither of us seems to mind.

We begin dating exclusively, and I soon learn that with Chris you get only the best. The best dining. The best wine. The best vacations. The best gifts — a bracelet from Tiffany, a Tag Heuer watch. The best seats at the U.S. Open.

But it's not his money that attracts me. I simply enjoy his company and the closeness we feel for each other. He's also the most selfless person I know. Kind and caring like no other. I genuinely love him.

We move in together in DUMBO, living in the lap of luxury on the twenty-first floor of a new high-rise overlooking the Brooklyn Bridge and downtown Manhattan. Sometimes we smoke weed and watch Godzilla movies or black-and-white Joan Crawford or Bette Davis films. We play Nintendo Wii and Xbox 360. And we constantly listen to music on our Apple TV.

My alcoholic tendencies continue to escalate. Alcoholism is a progressive disease, and I am increasingly upping the ante. Back in my AOL days, when I was going out almost every night, I would drink three or four beers. Now I'm cranking it up a notch to drinking a bottle of wine or six-pack a day. Chris can hold his liquor better than I can. I'm in outer space after one bottle of wine; he's still on Earth but just a bit buzzed. I ask myself, Am I a functioning alcoholic? To which I reply, Who cares?

As any nice couple would, we go to bed at the same time to cuddle or even to make love. But I'm getting to the point of preferring the bottle to sex. I stay up a couple of hours later than he does, drinking myself to oblivion most nights. I've been heavy-drinking for so many years that my hangovers have become manageable. All I need to get through the day is a coffee on the way to work and a few more to stay caffeinated through the work hours.

One New Year's Eve we opt for a quiet evening in. We cook filet mignon au poivre and potatoes au gratin, a rich and special dinner for the occasion. We stay up till midnight and watch the fireworks explode over the river.

After a sensual New Year's kiss, Chris goes to bed. I think he expects me to join him. We might have made love for the first time in 2007, which would have been romantic, but I'm hell-bent on getting drunker than I already am. I'm all fired up and decide to watch the *Alien* trilogy, which means I have six more hours of drinking ahead of me. I run out to the bodega for three six-packs. It's New Year's Eve, so my bulk purchase doesn't seem abnormal. I don't go to bed till 6 a.m.

But New Year's isn't the only time I stay up drinking well after Chris's gone to sleep, yet I'm too perpetually drunk to realize that this pattern of behavior is causing a rift between us. I can't admit to myself that I prefer spending quality time with the bottle, not my professed boyfriend.

Chris is a homebody, so it's tricky to get him out of the house unless it's for art or live music, which can range from the Metropolitan Opera or the New York Philharmonic to a jazz club. We'll always grab a quick beer or glass of wine during intermission. We drink any chance we can get. Many days, our teeth are purple.

I've never had a partner who appreciates the arts the way he does. We see the Takashi Murakami Japanese Pop Art exhibit as well as a retrospective on 1980s wunderkind and Andy Warhol protégé Jean Michel Basquiat, both at the Brooklyn Museum.

Rock 'n' roll is Chris's first love, but he also admires and enjoys all types of music. One night I come home and he's stretched out on the couch listening to Beethoven's "Moonlight Sonata." He's crying. I think it's beautiful.

Every Sunday, without fail, we alternate cooking dinner, during which we consume excessive amounts of wine. The recipes are time-intensive, so there's plenty of time to drink. We make elaborate dishes like boeuf bourguignon, Moroccan chicken tagine, or four-cheese lasagna with turkey Italian sausage. Dinner is followed by more drinks, weed, and all the good Sunday night TV — *The Simpsons*, *Dexter*, *True Blood*.

We take elaborate vacations to Anguilla in the British Virgin Islands, to Paris, to St. Lucia in the Caribbean, to Bali, Indonesia. While away we drink to excess every night. It's not unusual for us to polish off a bottle of Veuve Cliquot champagne while we're still on appetizers. Then it's on to another bottle, usually a sauvignon blanc, for the entrée. We never leave a drop behind and are beyond tipsy when we leave the restaurant. The next day we sightsee hungover and repeat the process.

In Bali, we visit temples and experience Hindu ceremonies, sober but hungover. The locals invite us to attend a funeral, so we get decked out in multi-hued batik sarongs and join the throngs of villagers dressed in all colors of the rainbow. It's so upbeat that it feels as if we're attending a wedding, not a funeral. The body of the deceased is placed in a large, decoratively painted wooden cow, which the townspeople parade through the street before gathering in the main square, where the cow will be burned, cremating the body. A dozen or so musicians loudly play drums, cymbals, and gamelans, and I wince from the noise. The music is so busy that it triggers auditory hallucinations, and the sound lingers between my ears well after the last musician has gone to sleep.

My few memories of our travels are blurry, time-lapse visions, indistinct moments blending into each other. Was that time we danced on the beach in the moonlight Bali, or was it the BVIs? Did we have our Best Meal Ever in Paris or St. Lucia? In some cases, I recall these facts as if they are someone else's memories, travelogues I've only read about, not actually experienced. The drinking has watered down my memories to the point that they exist as a nebulous cloud, a region of my mind that cannot be fully accessed, like the corrupt portion of a hard drive.

And my hard-core drinking hasn't even begun.

CHAPTER 7

BREAKING MAD

2007–2008

December 3, 2007: 2PM. I'm ruminating in a hotel room in Manchester, New Hampshire. It's four hours until show time for a live MTV production with then–presidential candidate John McCain, a Q&A with college students asking the questions. I'm producing Gideon Yago, a correspondent for MTV News, at Southern New Hampshire University, and we have some downtime before the big show.

I can't sit still. My palms gush with sweat. I wipe my hands on my jeans over and over and over again, but the sweat doesn't go away. I wash and dry my hands. Still sweating, I pace the room. There's nothing I can do. I'm trapped. Can't calm myself. I think I'm gonna die. I try to take a nap, but I only toss and turn. I go out in the cold every half hour to smoke. This is anxiety. Beyond normal anxiety. In fact, it's a panic attack. Live TV is the ultimate stressor.

I'm a shy person, although I always manage to overcome my shyness when work is involved. But here in New Hampshire my anxiety is winning the battle, and every time I think *We're going to be live* it only worsens, my throat constricting to the point where I feel I won't be able to gasp a final breath. The panic attack is so intense that as soon as I get back to New York I start seeing a psychiatrist, Anna, who diagnoses me with depression and prescribes Prozac, one pill a day.

The Prozac turns me around, and I feel incredibly good. Too good.

I don't need sleep. I stay up every night drinking copious amounts of wine and beer and also smoking weed, and sometimes I go to work on zero hours of sleep. I'm manic, a word whose meaning I don't yet know. A bona fide maniac.

* * *

On January 22, 2008, Heath Ledger dies of an overdose of psychotropic meds. I'm crestfallen. I'm not a huge fan, but as soon as I learn he was dealing with depression and was on the same drugs as I am, I feel a connection. Plus I'm still manic and hypersensitive. That night I watch *Brokeback Mountain* and have my own candlelight vigil in our living room. I pause the movie on a good still and take a picture of it with the candles burning on the TV stand. I email the picture to my coworkers. My boss takes notice and puts me on the case.

I travel to Carroll Gardens in Brooklyn, where Ledger and Michelle Williams have lived in a beautiful brownstone. The sidewalk is blanketed with flowers, notes, and tributes.

I take a zillion photos for a slideshow to go with my story. One bouquet has a note attached that reads "I served you at Brawta Café, your favorite, jerk chicken." I go to the Jamaican restaurant and interview the owner, who had left the flowers. I also interview mourners outside his other apartment, in downtown Manhattan, a somber scene where people are singing sad songs and lighting candles. I cry on the subway on the way back to work listening to "Someone Great," an LCD Soundsystem song about death. When the article is finished, my boss says it's some of my best work.

* * *

Manic becomes lunatic. I go to Philadelphia on a press junket promoting the city's music scene. I take the train from Penn Station. The high ceilings there cause voices to echo in my head to the point of annoyance. I've got my trusty composition book and start interviewing random people, telling them I'm writing a book about pop culture. One woman I meet works in the publishing industry and is impressed by my enthusiasm. She gives me her card and says, "Call me when you're ready to write your memoirs." I lose the card.

When I get to Philly, I'm absolutely fascinated by everything and everyone. I talk rapidly to strangers like they're my best friends. The other journalists must think I'm high or completely crazy. I go to a party hosted by Spank Rock, an up-and-coming rapper. Hipsters everywhere, and everyone is doing coke. I don't partake. I'm already high. Naturally.

The next day I go to a record store and buy a stack of vinyl a foot high. The records are bizarrely esoteric. I don't even know who most of the bands are. I make my selections based solely on how the cover art or titles make me feel.

Later that evening I hang out with Philadelphia DJ Diplo, a world-famous electronic-dance music producer. I monopolize Diplo for fifteen minutes, showing him my records on the way to a club. My manic brain has convinced me that I'm actually going to DJ there with my new records.

But when I arrive, the idea dissolves and I'm instead drawn to the dance floor. Diplo is quite the eccentric himself. He's brought colored construction paper and scissors to the club. He cuts out a yellow giraffe and gives it to me. I return to the dance floor and proudly trip the light fanatic with my construction-paper pal.

The next day I wander the city for hours, crying out of happiness as I listen on my iPod to Arcade Fire and The Teenagers, a French band I'm obsessed with and have running on a loop.

Back in New York, the madness continues. I move about in hyper speed. I think I'm on a reality show, that there are cameras in the apartment watching my every move. I ham it up for my imaginary audience, dancing around the living room with my iPod blasting, towel on my head, even though I showered hours ago. I rearrange furniture, books, and DVDs.

I walk around Times Square, overstimulated. I look up at the neon lights and billboards, hallucinating colors — especially purple, which I associate with change, à la the Obama campaign mantra

"Change we can believe in." I see purple everywhere I go. It pops out among the other colors, even when it's not there.

I go to work one morning and skip out around midday to wander the streets. I catch bits and pieces of conversation and think everyone is talking about me. It's fun at first. Then I get paranoid and it turns scary. Terrifying, even. Voices echo in my head, a jumble of verbal noise I can't decipher. My thoughts race like lasers.

I next go on a shopping spree at the Museum of Modern Art store and spend $200 on gifts for my coworkers, which I plan to leave on their desks after hours. I buy a Chicago Cubs baseball cap, even though I never wear hats and I'm not into sports. Then I head to Saks Fifth Avenue and max out my credit card on a $1,600 tailored Paul Smith suit and a $300 pair of sunglasses.

Returning to work loaded with shopping bags, I bump into Jason Segel, my biggest Hollywood crush, outside the building. He's smoking a cigarette. I startle him with my rapid-fire speech. I had fallen in love with him when he played a rock 'n' roll–obsessed character on *Freaks and Geeks*, the short-lived Judd Apatow–produced dramedy from the late '90s. I'm so high on my mania, I don't even remember what I've said to him when he excuses himself to go back inside. I scan my brain, trying to remember if what I've said was coherent or downright embarrassing, but the conversation is gone.

* * *

When you're manic, you overflow with ideas both good and bad. You think you're brilliant, but you're really just self-obsessed. I

69

come up with an idea for a blog I want to write for MTV News. The pitch is a meticulously crafted, cryptic, glorified PowerPoint presentation that lives online with its own domain and a soundtrack. I have spent almost every night for two months — while drinking and smoking pot — designing the ten-page online presentation. I call the project ConorTV, a play on MTV.

Befitting my manic egomania, the blog I propose would feature personal essays from me — and only me. I show the pitch to my boss, who is fazed and confused. Of course the pitch includes music by The Teenagers, my current obsession. When my pitch is rejected, I launch the blog on my own without permission at ConorTV.com. It has MTV iconography.

The Teenagers are a goofy indie-pop trio who specialize in crude lyrics about "fuckable" girls, Scarlett Johansson, greasy pizza, ketamine, spring break, and MySpace. The danceable music is quite catchy, and for some reason I connect to their debut album, *Reality Check,* on a profound level, to the point where I believe that lead singer Quentin Delafon is singing directly to me. Manic me sees a profound, concept-album character study on of-the-moment pop culture, but really it's just a satire on 21st-century high school and college life.

I am so intertwined with this album that I have it in my mind that the band's upcoming Brooklyn show is actually a launch party for ConorTV.com. I have been tweeting (from @ConorTV) at the band about it, telling them how a review of their show will be the inaugural post.

The Teenagers are the hottest ticket in New York City that spring. I coax six coworkers to come to the concert, held at the Music Hall of Williamsburg.

I show up on manic time — late — so I don't catch the opening act. But I'm just in time for the main event. I still believe this concert is being thrown in my honor and expect nothing less than pyrotechnics, champagne, and a big sheet cake with "ConorTV" emblazoned on it. It's the middle of the concert when I realize that no, this show is not dedicated to me.

I leave crestfallen and more than a little embarrassed. I am indeed scorching-hot motherfucking manic. I feel sick to my stomach as I hail a cab on North 6th Street. Another panic attack. I lie down in the backseat of the cab and sit up, lie down, sit up. I can't stay still. Home, I pop my meds and go to bed. Chris is asleep already. Thank God for Klonopin. I take three, triple my normal dose, and I'm out like a light.

* * *

In April my behavior has Chris so worried that he takes me to see Anna, my psychiatrist. After playing hooky from work, I hop over to Chris's nearby recording studio with the intention of noodling on his sky-blue Fender Jag-Stang guitar, the same style that was customized for Kurt Cobain. The plan is for me and Chris to take a cab to Anna's, but I ditch that plan and decide to walk, even though her office is thirty blocks away, on the Upper East Side.

On my way to Anna's office, I walk through Central Park, stopping people listening to their iPods to ask what they're listening to. I chat up a beautiful brunette from Belgium and learn she's listening to "Perfect Day," by Lou Reed. I think it's a sign — a message from the universe or some higher power.

I'm running on manic time again and so arrive at Anna's fifteen minutes late. Chris is already there. I take a seat next to him on the couch.

"Chris tells me you've been running amok," Anna says matter-of-factly. "How are you feeling?"

"I'm not running amok. I feel great," I reply. I feel accused and so put on the best façade I can muster. "Never been better. I've been super-productive at work, writing stories and cutting videos. My boss says I'm 'on fire' and that I'm doing a fantastic job. What's the problem?"

"'On fire' is an understatement," Chris says. "Ever since Conor got back from Philadelphia, he's been out of control."

"In what way?" Anna asks.

"That night, he completely ignored me. He danced around our apartment pumping his fist and waving a towel around in the air while listening to his iPod. The whole time I was thinking, *What drugs did they give him in Philadelphia?*"

Anna asks Chris to leave the room.

"Conor, I'm going to give you a new diagnosis," Anna says. "You're not depressed. You're manic. You have bipolar disorder."

I let it sink in. Bipolar. Manic. Yes, I've been acting erratically, I finally admit to myself.

She gives me a sample pack of Lamictal, a mood stabilizer. She also puts me on an antipsychotic. "I want to see you three times a week," she says.

* * *

Facebook and Twitter are dangerous when you're manic. Back on my laptop at home, I begin updating my Facebook status every five minutes. I write weird quips on my friends' Facebook walls and dedicate songs to friends and strangers via the music app iLike.

I'm still manic despite the new drugs. At MTV News, I write some of my best stories in this state. And my coworkers notice how happy I am. It's like I'm emanating happiness, and everyone is attracted to me because of it.

A few days later, I crash. I wake up and I can't get out of bed. My body feels heavy. I'm crying uncontrollably. I force myself to go to work, and the minute I get there I slam the door to my office and lose my shit. "Why are you crying?" my office-mate Michael says.

"Because George Bush ruined the world!" I say, apropos of nothing. I am visibly distraught, beyond typical sadness or crying. My eyes are bloodshot and my frown is pronounced. It's cemented on my face.

"Hang tight. I'll be right back." Michael swiftly leaves, then returns a few minutes later. He enters the office tentatively, as if there's a bomb inside and if he moves too quickly it'll explode. I am the bomb. "Are you OK, man?"

"No …" I pause a moment, unsure of how much to reveal, then suddenly burst out, "I'm bipolar!" It's the first time I've actually said

73

it out loud. The word is sandwiched between sobs. I can barely put together a sentence of more than a few words. When I do speak, it's guttural.

"Why don't you come with me?" Michael says softly as he holds out his hand to help me out of my desk chair. "Let's get you some help." Once I've stood up, he puts his hand on my shoulder and leads me toward the office of our boss, Adam. He guides me through the corridors as I walk, my gaze focused on the floor. Our office is dimly lit, and I feel as if I'm venturing through a cave.

"Hey, Conor!" I hear another coworker approach, and I know he's going to ask me about the shoot I'm supposed to have today with The Teenagers. He stops dead in his tracks, his question frozen on his opened lips when he sees my face. His expression conveys how bad a state I'm in.

Michael comes to my aid, saying, "Not now," and guides me away while my colleague stands gaping.

Once I'm in Adam's office, Michael leaves. My boss looks me up and down as he motions me to take a seat. He tries to seem calm, but I can tell my appearance has him rattled. "Michael tells me you were crying hysterically."

"Yes." It's an effort to say even the smallest of words. I wonder if I should tell my boss my diagnosis, if that will somehow affect my job status. But since I've already told Michael, Adam is bound to find out sooner or later. So I tell him. "I'm bipolar. I think I'm having a depressive episode."

Adam seems to take the news in stride. He tries his best to give me a reassuring smile, but it comes off like a grimace. "I'll get someone else to cover your shoot today. I think the best thing for us to do now is meet with human resources." In less than an hour I'm on medical leave for an undetermined length of time.

* * *

Medical leave isn't so bad. I use my newfound free time to visit museums, sleep in after a late night at a concert, and write. It's almost like being on vacation, and the anxiety I'd experienced at work is nowhere to be seen.

One day I hop on the F train to meet a friend in Manhattan. The train chugs along in a lulling cadence, to the point where I nearly fall asleep. A moment later, I bolt upright with the feeling that everyone is watching me. As I glance around the car, every eye seems to fix in my direction. Sweat builds on my forehead, and I feel like I won't be able to breathe if I stay down here.

I forget my plans and decide I have to get the fuck outta the subway, away from the prying eyes.

As soon as I exit at Broadway-Lafayette, I call my friend and former roommate Hank, now a German literature PhD student at Columbia University. I haven't seen him in months. He realizes I'm having a panic attack within seconds of picking up.

"Everything's gonna be OK. Just come to the Upper West Side," he says, trying to relay calmness and serenity over the phone line. "Take a taxi and I'll meet you on the steps at the Athena statue," he instructs, noting an iconic spot on the Columbia campus.

Once in the cab, I find myself in the same agitated state I'd been in after The Teenagers show. I can't sit still. I lie down, sit up, and repeat. I can't calm myself down.

When I meet Hank at Columbia, he decides we should go for a walk in Riverside Park. It's a beautiful spring day and I haven't eaten anything yet, so on the way we pick up bagels for a picnic.

As we walk to the park, I tell Hank everything there is to know about my diagnosis and my life over the past six months since I've seen him. He takes it all in, and there's no judgment in his voice as he begins to talk me down.

My heart is beating like a jackrabbit's, double the BPMs for a human being. I'm chain-smoking and twiddling and twitching my fingers in a nervous tic. I don't know what else to do with my hands, which shake uncontrollably, even when they're jammed tightly in my pockets.

We find a bench to sit on. The bagel is a good distraction. As I drink my orange juice and continue to spill my guts, a cool spring breeze from the nearby Hudson River rushes over us, mollifying my mood. We go for a walk along the river.

Hank just lending an ear is the greatest help. The mere act of walking and talking with him in the serenity of one of NYC's most beautiful parks is like psychotherapy between friends. My heart rate slows to normal. A sense of calm cascades throughout my body.

My hands stop shaking quite as badly. I've made it past another panic attack. *Buenísimo*.

* * *

Aside from that one panic attack, being on medical leave continues to feel like a kind of sabbatical. I'm not depressed anymore. I go to museums, walk across the Brooklyn Bridge, play Xbox 360 and Nintendo Wii. I write poetry. Really. Bad. Poetry. But in my manic state it sounds like Shakespeare, so I submit a poem to *The New Yorker*, thinking they might actually publish it. I get a rejection letter a few months later that reads, "We're sorry, we cannot use the enclosed materials." I don't take it personally.

Though I'm in a mixed state, crying one moment, ecstatic the next, hypomanic — a milder version of full-blown mania — at least the deep depression has subsided.

During this time I meet Augusten Burroughs at a signing in Bryant Park. I don't find it ironic that my favorite book of his is *Dry*, which chronicles his struggle with alcoholism. I'm talking laser speed, like I'm giving an elevator pitch, as I tell him he's one of my biggest influences as a writer. "I totally love you and I totally wanna be you and I'm writing my own memoir and it's about pop culture and bipolar disorder and you're my hero and will you read it when it comes out?" He signs my copy of *Wolf at the Table* without responding or meeting my eye. He probably thinks I am creepy.

After a month on sick leave I get back to work thinking I'm OK, but I break down crying hard again the moment I swipe my access card. I force myself to push forward and make it up the elevator to my floor. Still looking disheveled, I do my best to avoid coworkers, but I run into one of the on-air talent, Tim Kash, who asks in his British accent where I've been.

"I've been out for personal reasons," I say, trying to avoid eye contact.

"Personal reasons," he repeats, and leaves it at that.

Once back in my office, I distract myself by reading blogs and researching story ideas. Somehow I manage to make it through the day. The next day is better. Frequent walks around the block help.

I'm so depressed that I've actually stopped drinking. I can feel the depression intensify with each sip, just making things worse. I cry every day for almost a year.

Anna experiments with various medications and doses to find the right cocktail for me. I'm stockpiling pill bottles. There are instances where she changes the dose and I don't need the previous bottle but I still keep the half-full bottles around, "just in case." I tell myself I'm keeping them in the event that I might need them again. But really I know I won't need them for therapeutic purposes, because I'm hoarding ones I don't even tolerate. It becomes an obsession. I'm saving the pills for a "rainy day."

The first antipsychotic my doctor prescribes is Abilify. My first night on it, I take my meds before bed and vomit thirty minutes later. It's more like "Disabilify" for me. I still keep the bottle, yet another trophy in my plastic menagerie of pill bottles.

Anna experiments with every antidepressant under the sun, and it takes a year to find the right combo. She finally tries lithium, which works to stabilize my moods.

When the Bush recession hits, MTV News lays off about twenty people, and I'm one of them. I get drunk that night with coworkers at an Irish pub near our office, just off Times Square. I'm not distraught about the layoff. If anything, I figure that given my multifarious moods, mostly bad, over the past year, I could use a reprieve.

Chris breaks up with me as soon as I get stable, which is shortly after the layoffs. He says something like, "Things have just started to feel ... *routine*." I have a hunch it has more to do with the fact that we never have sex when I'm depressed or that my previous drunken night-owl tendencies haven't gelled with a sexual relationship.

I move into a one-bedroom in Carroll Gardens, where I isolate myself from my friends. Within a few months I've squandered my severance on beer and wine. What starts as a six-pack or bottle of wine per night slowly turns into two six-packs, sometimes three. I'm longing for the mania, and being drunk feels almost like it.

Thanks to Nate, the same friend who hooked me up with the MTV job, I land a short-term gig covering the Tribeca Film Festival for AMC. I stop drinking for the duration of the five-day festival, but I feel dazed and distracted. Feebleminded and dopey. Barely capable of doing my job.

I've got the shakes, which are compounded by my nervousness and overall anxiety at being in a high-stress situation. When

I interview Robert De Niro at a press junket, I'm told I have five minutes with him. But I'm in such a terrible state that I don't even use the full time, and running out of questions, I get flustered. I can't improvise. "That's it?" De Niro says to me.

"I guess so," is my lame reply.

I am officially the worst interviewer ever. I kick myself for wasting such an opportunity. Trying to salvage something out of this train wreck, I vow to come to any future interviews with far more questions than I'll ever need. I've already known this, of course, but my anxiety has thrown me for a loop and caused me to jettison even my most basic journalism skills.

Much of the rest of the assignment involves red-carpet interviews, which are far more stressful than regular live TV. First off, you have to be quick to recognize the celebrities, who are parading past you in droves and are being courted by dozens of other media. If you succeed in calling a celebrity over, you have only a few seconds to fire off your questions, and since there's no way you can know who will come over to you, it's not like you can refer to a prepped list. Once you've snared a celeb, the goal is to keep them talking as long as possible. I'm pretty certain the stress level is just one below air-traffic controller.

I'm also trying to simultaneously flash my microphone, emblazoned with the AMC logo, and hide it, since my hands are shaking so much the crew is giving me strange looks. But somehow I make it through the day and land interviews with Kirsten Dunst, Joan Rivers, and Renée Zellweger.

I celebrate the end of the assignment by getting mind-wastingly blotto. My drinking routine continues the very next day. And only gets worse.

CHAPTER 8

MY ALCOHOLIC ROMANCE

2009

The Chicago Dragons rugby team is hosting the Rockford Ravens on this fine fall afternoon. The Dragons are the gay team in the league, and I'm dating Jeffrey, who plays for it. Since we've begun seeing each other, I've learned a lot about the sport. For example, unlike in American football, there are no pads or helmets in rugby.

After the game, we head to the North End, a gay sports bar in Boystown, where I experience the insanity of my first rugby party. It's like a frat party but with even more camaraderie. And even more drinking.

A ginger guy, who's been given the very original nickname of Red, jumps up on the pool table to lead us in a call-and-response song, which I soon learn is a rugby tradition. Like everyone in the room, he's holding a plastic cup of beer. He *owns* that pool table like it's a stage and he's the star.

RED: Thursday is a drinking day!

EVERYONE: Thursday is a drinking day!

RED: Friday is a fucking day!

EVERYONE: Friday is a fucking day!

SATURDAY'S A RUGBY DAY!!! SATURDAY'S A RUGBY DAY!!! SATURDAY'S A RUGBY DAY!!! SATURDAY'S A RUGBY DAY!!!

RED: And Sunday … is the Lord's day.

He kneels on the pool table as the rest of the room bursts into applause.

Later, there's a guy stripping down to his birthday suit. He's the lucky man who scored his first try (point) ever. After being forced to chug a beer, he heads for the exit and runs around the block stark naked. When he gets back, he has to chug another beer. Then he has to score a bull's-eye — or close enough — on the dartboard before he can put his clothes back on.

This party is an alcoholic's dream come true.

I discover that rugby has a rich history of drinking traditions, and that draws me to Jeffrey even more. I want to be a part of this society of debauchery, a place where my drinking is not only accepted but encouraged.

I start dating Jeffrey shortly after I move back into my parents' apartment in Chicago, which I do in 2009 because I can no longer afford my Carroll Gardens place. We drink every time we get together, even when we're not at rugby parties.

While others are ironically drinking PBR, we prefer craft beers before they're all the rage. We're early adopters. Beer aficionados. Whether it's a Belgian white in the summer or pumpkin ale in the fall, a chocolate stout in the winter or a farmhouse ale in the spring, we have brews for all seasons. We always drink specialty beers. Except when we're cheap and buy a thirty-pack of Budweiser.

As with Chris, I meet Jeffrey on gay.com. On your profile, you can list your drinking preferences. His said, "Drinks lots." I have to admit it was one reason I contacted him in the first place.

When I drink, I am jovial. Get a few beers in me and I'm beaming with joy. I smile and laugh. I'm goofy. I love the part of me that comes alive when I've knocked back a few beers, the person who emerges with each subsequent sip. It's as if the alcohol erodes the shell that's been hiding the real me, and I'm further bolstered by the energy from everyone I interact with. They love me.

It's the opposite when Jeffrey drinks.

Jeffrey is a Republican, and we have many a fight about politics. And by fight, I do not mean civil discourse. I mean screaming matches. He becomes belligerent when drunk. He refers to the president as "Barack Hussein Obama" and accuses me of having an unhealthy obsession with No. 44. He uses Rush Limbaugh talking points.

On one of our first dates, Jeffrey and I drink for a solid ten hours, sleep, and then get up for breakfast, when we have Irish coffee and then go out day-drinking at a dive bar in Boystown. We basically drink for twenty-four hours, minus sleep.

I make mixtapes for him, and he is quite the music fan as well. We dance by the jukebox at dive bars if a particular song strikes our fancy. And we almost never have sex. Instead, we drink. We're drinking buddies.

One fall night, about fourteen months into our relationship, I down about twenty beers at Jeffrey's apartment. He goes to bed and I stay up later, drinking on the outside backstairs to enjoy the pleasant fresh air of the autumn night. I run out of beer, so I steal one from Jeffrey's roommate to make it a nice round twenty-one.

When I get up to go inside to bed, I trip and bang my head on the edge of a wooden pillar. I slice my forehead open — huge gash.

I bleed all over the apartment, leaving splotches and streaks of red on the walls and in the bathroom, where I'm thinking I can just wash it off and no one will be the wiser. Jeffrey hears me stumbling and gets up to see what's going on. When he sees the blood, he calls an ambulance. I don't know how many stiches I get, but the scar is two inches long.

My mom and dad happen to be in town when this happens, a fact that may be contributing to my excessive drinking. When I'm hanging out with them, I don't get to drink as much, so when I'm not with them, I make up for lost time and ingest all the alcohol I can.

I return around midday to find my mom in my apartment. When she asks what's happened to my forehead, I tell her I fell down some stairs at Jeffrey's. A few hours later, she takes me to see our regular family doctor, who says I also have a broken nose. They hadn't noticed at the ER.

The next night I'm back at Jeffrey's, stitches crisscrossing my forehead, a bandage on my nose, and a cold brewski in my hand. "You're hardcore," Jeffrey's roommate says. I just smile and take another swig of my beer.

Even though our relationship lasts for more than a year, I'm not in love with Jeffrey. I'm in love with the bottle.

And pill collecting. Now a couple of years into my bipolar diagnosis, I've accumulated an alphabet soup of various doses of Abilify, Ativan, Geodon, Klonopin, Lamictal, lithium, Paxil, Propanolol, Prozac, Seroquel, Vicodin, Wellbutrin, Xanax, maybe more. Definitely enough to kill myself. They all live under the bathroom sink in the biggest Ziploc bag you can buy.

And despite my love for getting high, it's becoming repetitive. Drinking can be fun, but it affects your mood over time. And by this point, five years into heavy drinking, I'm in a perpetually depressed funk, exacerbated by the constant flow of alcohol in my system. I've become stuck in a pattern, one from which there is no escape. I know that if I stop I'll probably feel better, but I don't feel capable of cleaning myself up. I am a slave to the routine.

One night, after a particularly vicious, alcohol-fueled fight with Jeffrey, I slink home and dig out the pills from under the bathroom cabinet. I decide I'm going to swallow all of those pills, washing them down with my precious Blue Moon. I line up the prized bottles on my coffee table — my treasures — and ponder the situation. I've heard somewhere that one in four suicides happen when the person is drunk, and even though I know the reason I've been stockpiling all these pills, now that I'm here, I'm not sure I want to go through with it. Plus, as I've said, I'm a procrastinator.

Despite being close to blind with drunkenness, I manage to find the number to the National Suicide Prevention Lifeline. The only reason I know I've called them is because the next morning when I awaken, still in a drunken fog, I see the number listed in my outgoing calls on my cell phone. I can't recall a single word of our conversation, but I have a glimmer of recollection that I called.

All I know is, that phone number saved my life — and on more than one occasion. I call the hotline three other times in the next several weeks. At least, that's what my phone says.

And as much as those calls help me, they're not enough. I begin seeking out higher highs to counter my depressive lows. This is when I begin frequenting the Palace of Debauchery. It's my lowest low yet.

CHAPTER 9

THE INTERVENTION

January 2012

Winter has been clobbering Chicago, but today we're getting a break with a beautiful springlike fifty-seven degrees.

Instead of enjoying the unusual weather, I'm holed up in my apartment, drinking a tallboy of Miller High Life. It's becoming my preferred beverage because it's cheap. And of course it's "the Champagne of Beers." If the weather holds up, this evening will be quite pleasant. I plan to spend it, as I do every evening I'm not with Jeffrey, at the Palace of Debauchery, smoking crack with John. I'm looking forward to the warm night breeze under the stars while we sit on the loading dock. A crack pipe sizzling under a yellow moon. The image alone makes me happy.

As usual, the apartment is a mess. Empty wine bottles on the counter. Crushed beer cans all over the place. Trash can topped off. Dirty clothes blanketing the bedroom floor. Dust everywhere. I couldn't care less.

There's a knock on the door. No one ever knocks except the building's Mr. Fix-It. I open up and am shocked to find my dad bundled up in winter clothes, ones he wouldn't have brought with him from Maui.

My dad barely comes inside. He's stiff and clearly angry. "I'm here because we have to address your situation," he says, his voice taking a stern tone so foreign to me it sounds as if someone else is speaking. "We're going to have a family meeting to talk about your drinking. It's going to be one week from today in the apartment at 10AM. I have nothing more to say. We'll talk then."

He leaves.

I feel invaded. Nervous. Nauseated. I pick up my cell and call Anna, who is still in New York but continues to counsel me via phone. Anna is the one who diagnosed me with bipolar, so I feel a particular bond, as if she alone truly gets me. I also know she'll defend me no matter what. And she'll help me get through this — whatever *it* is.

She returns my call within minutes. Anna never leaves me waiting.

I tell her about my dad's visit, and she begins to calm me down with her usual pragmatic tone. "I know you must be scared," she says. "I want you to remember that you are your own person. This is what we've been working on. You're an adult. No one can make you do anything you don't want to do." She asks when the meeting will take place. "I suggest you take your meds and get some sleep. Take an extra Xanax if you need to. We'll talk again tomorrow."

That night, Jeffrey comes over to calm me down some more. And by "calm me down," I mean bring me wine. I start to feel better as the alcohol courses through my veins, tingly and soothing.

But then the night leads where it always does: to Jeffrey and me fighting over politics. This soon turns to the subject I don't want to discuss, which is whether or not my dad's visit means my family is going to try to convince me to go to rehab. Jeffrey doesn't think I should go, but I know he's only saying that because he'll lose his drinking buddy, not because he actually cares how bad my drinking is. Just to spite him, I tell him I'm going, although I have absolutely no intention of doing so.

We scream at each other like we've never screamed before. We're so loud and it's so late that I'm surprised the neighbors don't call the cops. The argument gets increasingly heated until Jeffrey just stops, grabs the remote, and puts on "The End" by The Doors. He glares at me meaningfully.

It is indeed the end. I was already fishing for a reason to commit suicide, and the impending family meeting and now the breakup are reasons enough. I go into the bathroom, slam the door, and take a fistful of lithium. Lithium can fuck up your kidneys.

Jeffrey rams the door, bursts in, and stops me before I have time to dip further into my menagerie of pill bottles. When he sees the empty lithium bottle, he calls an ambulance.

At Northwestern Memorial Hospital, they pump my stomach. It doesn't hurt because I'm so numb from the alcohol. At least I don't need dialysis, although the doctor says I was pretty close. I end up being admitted for two days. For months, no one other than Jeffrey knows about my botched suicide attempt. And he destroys the evidence when he flushes the entire contents of the Ziploc bag down the toilet.

When I get out of the hospital, I resume my talks with Anna, whom I don't tell about the suicide attempt. I'm too ashamed, even though she's the one I'm supposed to tell everything to. There are the usual adjustments in medications to address my upset state. I'm on a mish-mash of meds: lithium, Lamictal, Geodon, Xanax, Propanolol, Prozac. I up my dose on the Prozac.

The family meeting is just days away, so to prepare I limit my drinking and thoroughly clean the apartment. I don't want them to see how I've been living. I need to rid the place of evidence and make myself as presentable as possible. I don't need to give them any more ammunition.

Anna has advised me how to handle the meeting, which I'm slowly beginning to realize is, in fact, an intervention. I've also had another realization, one about my recent visit with my parents in Maui for Christmas. My father had asked me to meet a friend of his for coffee, but when I got there all I wanted to do was take off; the guy just kept talking about the twelve steps and how freaking great it was to finally be sober. It didn't register with me at the time that my father had arranged this meeting to try to get me to see I had a problem. Instead, all I could think as this random surfer dude with sleeve tattoos rambled on was that I was nothing like him, that his problems weren't mine. It isn't until now, as the "family meeting" looms before me, that I recognize that my coffee with surfer dude was my parents' first attempt at an intervention. Either I had been in too much denial or was just too blitzed for it to register. Anna asks me again about my drinking, and as always I lie and assure her that it's under control. "Once in a blue moon, I'll have a beer," I tell her, pleased with myself for the sly reference to my favorite brand without her picking up on it. I don't mention that I've become a back-alley crackhead. As far as I'm aware, no one — not even Jeffrey — knows about the drugs. But part of me wonders if someone's figured it out, and that's why they've called this intervention. My stomach churns at the thought, so I pop a Xanax and pass out for a few hours. My dreams are as bad as my reality.

On the day of the meeting, the temperature has dropped back to freezing. Four inches of fresh snow lie on the ground. I open my front door to find a perfect stranger on my doorstep. He looks like Steve Jobs, with his shiny bald head and metal-frame glasses. "Conor, my name is Neil Haverford. I often help families have discussions like the one you're about to have." He says this as cheerfully as if we're about to throw an ice cream party, not put me on trial.

I invite him in and offer coffee as he shares what his role will be and who will be attending. He's calm and composed, while my anxiety has my body jittering so much I practically spill the contents of my cup. Neil tells me my parents arranged weeks ago for him to be here today.

Colleen and my dad arrive and, aside from a perfunctory greeting, say nothing until Neil signals it's time to begin. I sit Indian-style on the floor, coffee mug clenched in both hands. I could squeeze myself in between my dad and sister on the couch, but I prefer to keep my distance. So I've unwittingly put myself in a situation where everyone is, literally and figuratively, looking down on me.

My palms are sweating. Despite my attempts to clean myself up, I'm gaunt and pale. Anxious. Unkempt. I'm doing my best to avoid eye contact. My hands vibrate like guitar strings ringing out at the end of a song. They shake in any case as a side effect of the lithium, but when I'm nervous it gets worse.

Neil places the phone in the middle of us all so that Anna and my mom, both on speakerphone, can better hear. "Help me understand what's going on," Neil says to start us off. "Why are we here now?"

My dad takes the reins. "I don't even know how to begin," he says, already tearing up. "I'm so upset. My feelings are deep and they make me want to cry." He turns to my sister. "Colleen has been saying you are an alcoholic for a long time. Your mom and I just couldn't come to believe it. But now we do."

It kills me to see the pain on my dad's face. I've barely ever seen him cry.

"You're not the person we know," he continues, trying to maintain his composure. From time to time, he runs his fingers through his gray hair, a gesture he makes when he's nervous or uncomfortable. "You look out of it all the time. You stare into space. And there was that time you cut your forehead and broke your nose falling downstairs. We finally put two and two together and realized you did that while drinking. All signs point to alcoholism." He voice gets strained as he adds, "You are killing yourself." He puts his head in his hands while Colleen comforts him.

My mom uses the pause to jump in. "We're very worried about you," she says, blasting staccato on the speakerphone. "We think you're drinking way too much and it's dangerous with all the drugs you're on. This is something you can't solve yourself, and we have ideas we think can help."

Then Anna's voice overpowers my mom's. "I've been working with Conor since 2007," Anna says, her voice tinged with belligerence. "We've been working on some issues, but alcohol is not one of them."

I catch my dad and Colleen exchange glances. My sister has never been an Anna fan, so I can only assume she's told my parents that I need to get a better shrink, and Anna's ignorance of the extent of my drinking only furthers Colleen's agenda. No one in this intervention knows the true extent of my drinking, or that just days earlier I lay in a hospital bed under suicide watch. I wonder what they would be saying if they knew the full story.

Then Colleen says something that stuns me even as it fills in some pieces of the puzzle. I learn that the clan has been scheming about this intervention since Christmas, when I visited my parents in Maui. Colleen had used the opportunity to sneak into my apartment and retrieve some of my dad's clothes in preparation for his visit this week. But it wasn't just Colleen who got an eyeful. When my five-year-old nephew Peter saw — and probably smelled — the state of my apartment, he looked up at her and said, "Mommy, I don't want to come to Conor's apartment anymore." My recent cleaning had been for naught. Everyone already knew just what a sty I lived in.

When my dad brings up the subject of Alcoholics Anonymous, Anna steps up to my defense. "I've been counseling Conor to take ownership of his life. I've been helping him build up his confidence," she says, almost defensively. "I have to say, the relationship between you and Conor is … complicated. Sometimes you treat him like a child. He's an adult. If Conor opts to go to AA, that's something he has to decide on his own."

I don't agree with everything Anna says, but I'm not about to contradict the only person on my side. Sure, I'm open with my parents. I see them as friends, peers even. Since losing my job, I've been dependent on them financially, which in turn has made me more forthcoming with even private matters — except, of course, my substance abuse. In some ways, I consider my transparency as tit for their monetary tat.

"That may be," my mom counters, her voice growing sterner, "but he's not taking action. He needs to be pushed in the proper way. That's why we've hired a specialist to have this meeting. We want Conor to know how important this is, how dangerous what he's doing is. We don't want Conor to die. He's our son." She has trouble getting out the last part and I realize that my family has probably already discussed the possibility of my death. I'm torn between hating them for talking about me behind my back and shame for having made them think that at all.

Neil agrees that it's my choice whether or not to go to rehab or AA. They can't make me. "We're just here to express our concerns," he says. "Essentially, the ball is in Conor's court."

I don't say a word, continuing to listen but silently hoping this will end soon so I can be alone and pop open a beer. My sole contribution thus far has been to stare into my coffee mug. At least no one has even hinted at drugs so far.

"You were so disconnected when you were in Hawaii over Christmas," my dad says. "After you left, we learned you were down at the beach drinking every day. You became best friends with the bartenders. They all ask about you."

"You're not remembering things," Colleen interrupts. "One time you called me on Thanksgiving and we had a whole conversation about what you made for dinner. Then you called me an hour later and it was like we'd never talked. You didn't remember our previous conversation at all. Now when your name shows up on caller ID, I'm afraid to talk to you." I expect her to roll her eyes and chastise me for wasting her time. But her next words surprise me. "It's too painful."

"What is this, Dump on Conor Day?" I practically spit out the words, speaking for the first time since the intervention began. It's as if my family called this meeting just to point out my faults, how many times I've fucked up over the last several years. I'm just thankful they don't know about the drugs. If they did, Colleen would have mentioned it by now.

"No, Conor, we're just trying to help," my dad says, softening his voice. "You're destroying your mind and body. You don't even have a career anymore. You're a talented writer and you're just throwing it all away."

Colleen then brings out a picture of us in Central Park from two years earlier. It's of her, my mom, my three-year-old nephew, and me posing behind a Peter Rabbit statue.

"This is what you used to look like," she says in a quivering voice. "You were so alert." Out come the tears. "You look nothing like this photo now. Your eyes are always blurry. You smell like alcohol even when you try to hide it. I know, Conor; I can tell you try. It doesn't work. Even Peter asks, 'What's wrong with Uncle Conor?' A five-year-old knows. He's five!" She breaks down sobbing. "Look at this photo," she says, thrusting the picture in my face. "That's the brother I love. That's the brother I miss. I don't even recognize the smelly bag of bones in front of me."

She's right. I haven't been eating. But I'm doing a fuck of a lot of drinking. And despite my feeble attempt at hygiene, there are probably alcohol vapors emanating from my pores from last night's binge. "Smelly bag of bones" may sound harsh, but it is far kinder than the truth.

I say no more during the first session of my intervention, just drink my coffee and listen. When we finish, I agree to go to an assessment at the Chicago location of Hazelden Betty Ford.

Day two of my intervention is more of the same. I'm quiet but much less anxious, knowing pretty much what to expect and now relatively certain the drugs aren't going to be brought up. We go around the room, and everyone explains how alcohol has affected our relationships. Apparently, I also drunk-dial my parents.

"When you called us incoherent at three o'clock in the morning, it made us very upset," my dad says. "At first we thought that such a late call meant there was an emergency, someone had been hurt. Then we realized you were drunk. Loaded, actually."

I learn that I have been sending nasty drunk texts to everyone in my immediate family. Texts I don't remember. I'm drunk-communicating in most every medium I can think of. I've probably tweeted horrible things to them, even though neither is on Twitter.

"When I got to Chicago this week," my dad continues, "I was so angry at you. Not for having to come out here. But for *why* I had to come here." My dad is also a writer, so he chooses his words carefully when he continues. "If I'd come to help you move or celebrate a birthday or even just because you wanted me to visit, that would be one thing. But I had to come because you screwed up. We've given you every opportunity, and you're throwing it all away. I couldn't even be with you, until this meeting. I had to get away." He looks around the room as if he'll burst into tears again if he has to look me in the face. "After I left you last week, I took a train to New Orleans. I didn't stay there more than a few hours before I came back. I just needed to be anywhere that wasn't here, that wasn't near you." As if realizing his last words might have been unduly unkind, he adds, "I got books on bipolar and alcoholism for the train ride. I read AA stuff. I wanted to be as prepared as possible, to do everything in my power to help my son."

The whole point of this intervention is to get me to agree to go to rehab, and the pressure is mounting and doesn't look like it will stop, so at end of this second day I say, "I'll think about it." That's all they get out of me.

When they're finally out the door and the apartment is mine once again, I heave a sigh of relief, pop open a Miller High Life, then head out to join John at the Palace of Debauchery. As we fire up the crack pipe, we have a good laugh over how worried my family is about my drinking.

* * *

A couple of weeks later, I get the results of my Hazelden assessment. The doctor recommends the intensive outpatient program, or IOP, as it's known in recovery parlance. But I'm still hedging and won't commit to going, even though my parents call every day with a new angle to plead their case.

We reconvene for the third and final day of the intervention. When my sister hears the assessment, she drops the bomb. Not just some pitiful pipe bomb, but a weapon of mass destruction that makes me feel down-in-the-dumps depressed and dejected.

"Go to rehab or you can't see my son anymore."

Not "your nephew" but "my son."

To be honest, I'm not very close with my nephew. I play Legos with him, but I'm not enthusiastic about it. The whole time I'm just thinking about when I can crack open my next beer.

But when faced with the possibility of not being able to see him again, I realize I don't want to miss out on Peter's life. I've already planned to buy him an electric guitar for his thirteenth birthday and to pay for lessons at the Old Town School of Folk Music. I want to teach him about music, especially rock 'n' roll.

I become aware that I've been looking forward to these bonding moments with Peter more than I thought. Now the prospect of not seeing these dreams realized hits harder than all the berating I've endured over the last two sessions. Even my parents' tears haven't had this effect on me. Sure, they've made me feel like the world's crappiest son, but I can live with that. What I can't live with is Peter growing up thinking of me as the loser "drunkle" he hasn't seen since he was five.

Colleen isn't crying this time. She's agitated, to be sure, but there are no waterworks. An unfair ultimatum? Perhaps. But it works.

After a few seconds of silence, I say, "OK. I'll go."

But if I'm going to go to rehab, I first need a final, celebratory send-off. When no one shows up to party with me at the Palace of Debauchery, I spend the night in an alleyway high on crack and making out with a homeless guy.

As I head out the door to Hazelden the next afternoon, I realize that I probably should have done this sooner.

CHAPTER 10

REHAB

February 2012

February 6: day one of rehab. Hazelden is just a ten-minute walk down the street from me. The building is an old red-brick mansion in Chicago's posh Gold Coast neighborhood that looks like it could be on the National Register of Historic Places.

They give me a breathalyzer test and I blow a zero. After filling out some paperwork, I'm given a heap of reading material, including *A Man's Way Through the Twelve Steps*, *The Little Red Book*, and of course the bible, *Alcoholics Anonymous*, before joining my group. Although Hazelden isn't officially an AA entity, it does adhere to the twelve-step approach and encourages everyone to attend AA meetings.

Our meeting room feels like the private library of an affluent lawyer and exudes a warm glow. A richly colored carpet masks our footsteps on the hardwood floors. But there's one object that feels out of place amid all this coziness: Looming over us is an enormous poster of the twelve steps in a font so large it seems to be shouting like a drill sergeant with a bullhorn.

We meet for three hours four nights a week, six weeks total. The house is also a residence for the handful of people deemed in need of around-the-clock treatment. We're lucky that we get to leave each day.

Our addiction counselor, Tony, an attractive thirtysomething Italian-American, is so clean cut he could be a game-show host, and he has the same bubbly demeanor. He leads the discussions as we all sit in a circle. Crosstalk is allowed.

Tony begins every session the same way: "Who wants to start? Tell me your highs and lows."

I'm always more than willing to share my highs, which don't seem as soul baring. The group gets a kick out of the fact that one of my highs is having found a pair of fuzzy blue-plaid sneakers resembling a flannel shirt that had been lost in the shuffle of my drunken days.

Over the course of the first week, I become friends with Kate, a divorced lesbian with short-cropped hair who looks like a Wicker Park hipster and rides her racing bike everywhere, even in the ice and snow. Part of our bond is due to the fact that we're both gay.

I also befriend Tom, a former frat boy and current golfer and tennis player who works in finance and is obsessed with The Dave

Matthews Band. I abhor The Dave Matthews Band, and fraternity culture rubs me the wrong way, so I wouldn't have associated with Tom under any other circumstances.

He's received an acoustic guitar for Christmas, and I offer to teach him some basic chords and songs. I teach him "Wild Thing," by The Wild Ones, the easiest song I know on guitar. It's only three chords. We meet three or four times at my apartment for lessons and even play tennis that summer. My childhood lessons finally prove useful.

Monica is a graphic designer, so we have a natural common interest in all things creative. She runs her own business, designing logos, websites, et al. In fact, she designs my first website, promoting me as an author.

About two weeks into my treatment, Monica glances around the circle of now-familiar faces and says, "Something's different today. We all look so healthy, don't we?" Everyone agrees.

I'm reluctant to admit it at first, but I feel better too. My mind is much clearer. I don't have trouble remembering what I've done the day before. My appetite has returned to the point that I've begun eating regular meals again, even if it's just takeout. Jeffrey and I have broken up, but I feel relief rather than sadness, particularly since I've come to realize how toxic and enabling our relationship was. I've also been treating myself to some new music from the iTunes store, like the 30th Anniversary Deluxe Edition of The Go-Go's' *Beauty and the Beat*. Rediscovering music reawakens a part of me I hadn't realized was dormant.

Every time I hear a classic track, my heart leaps with joy, an emotion that only a few weeks ago I thought I might never feel again.

Rehab is working.

And it's surprisingly fun. Ten different personalities in one room. People who would never meet in the outside world. Everyone from businesspeople to creative types. Although we each start our treatment on different weeks, we quickly build bonds and are sad when one of us "graduates" out.

I'm usually hesitant to reveal my bipolar, especially with strangers or new acquaintances. But toward the end of the first week, the headspace of therapy helps me open up. "I'm feeling down today," I say. "No highs. I tried drinking nonalcoholic beer last night. It tastes vile. I vomited in the kitchen sink. I'm bored. I miss my friend beer. I'm depressed."

The group is sympathetic. No one else struggles with major depression, but everyone misses their drink of choice. Molly, the gray-haired grandma of the group, reminisces about her nightly concoction of Häagen Dazs coffee ice cream and Jameson Irish Whiskey. Everyone virtually drools.

Tony urges us never to drink "nonalcoholic" beverages, because despite their name they actually contain a tiny percentage of alcohol, which I didn't know. I vow to never try it again. It's disgusting anyway.

The group assures me that if I ever need to talk to someone, I'm welcome to call. We have a phone list.

I thank them and wonder if today is the day I'll reveal my drug use. Even in this "safe space," I still haven't admitted that part of my story to anyone outside the Palace of Debauchery. But when I next speak, I simply continue where I'd left off. "I have depression. Actually, I have bipolar disorder, but part of that is depression," I say. I let the words hang in the air to see what sort of reaction they elicit. I half expect to see people recoil in horror, or at least give me a sideways glance. But no one seems taken aback, so I continue. "Sometimes I can't get out of bed. I feel heavy. And deeply, deeply sad."

"Well, you made it here today," Tony chimes in. "That is an incredible, giant step."

"I know," I say. "And I feel better now that I'm here. It's just finding the motivation. And my doctor and I upped the Prozac."

"You shouldn't be on antidepressants," Ted, a certified nurse, says combatively. You would think that being in the medical profession, he would empathize. "If you want to be truly sober, you shouldn't be taking any drugs whatsoever. You should be a hundred-percent clean."

There's a faction of AA that believes taking medication for mood disorders disqualifies you from being sober. This is the first time I've ever been told this malarkey, and I can't believe I'm hearing it. It seems counterintuitive to everything I've learned about my bipolar condition. "Nonsense," I say, clearly annoyed. "My disease is real. In fact, I have two diseases. I follow the advice of my doctor, and she says I need these pills."

Ted looks as if he's about to start an argument, so Tony calls a timeout. "Drop time." He points to me and Monica. "You guys are up."

Every week we are subjected to a urine test — known in rehab circles as a "drop"— to see if we're taking any illicit drugs. My very first shows up positive for benzodiazepines, which are tranquilizers such as Valium, Klonopin, Ativan, and Xanax, which I'm on. Benzos have addictive properties.

At our next meeting, Tony pulls me aside to chat in a small conference room while the rest of the group watches a video about recovery. He has the results of our drops. "You can't go to Hazelden if you're on benzos," he says. "It's against our policy." I assure him that I don't abuse the Xanax. I take one pill at bedtime for insomnia, as prescribed.

The AA literature I've read so far says that some AA members do require medication, including those with suicidal depression and bipolar, among other ailments. At the beginning of every meeting, someone reads the following: "We ask that when discussing our problems, we confine ourselves to those problems as they relate to alcoholism." In other words, you're not supposed to talk about your feelings unless they jibe with your alcoholism. And feelings are what make us who are dually diagnosed tick.

Fortunately, in our group therapy, the rules about feelings are relaxed. I use our time together to vent. And I feel better every time.

But there is also a culture of conservatism in the rooms of AA. Those of us with mood disorders are ostracized. Many AA adherents believe you're poisoning your body with chemicals if you take prescription meds, that pills of any kind are agents of contamination, and that you can't *truly* be clean if you are on meds of any kind. Just follow the twelve magical steps of the program, and all your problems will be cured.

"I'm on a very complex regimen of medication for my bipolar," I say to Tony. "Can't you talk to my doctor?" I give him Anna's number. We agree to meet after their conversation.

A couple of days later, I arrive at Hazelden for my one-on-one with Tony. As I pour myself a cup of coffee in the lobby, my hands shake so viciously that I'm spilling it everywhere. Visibly nervous, I walk up the stairs to Tony's office and run into Tom in the stairwell.

"You got the shakes?" Tom asks, referring to the tremors associated with alcoholic withdrawal. He carries my coffee upstairs for me.

When I enter Tony's office, he immediately notices how jittery and flustered I am. "I don't know if you should be drinking that coffee, man," Tony says. He does me the favor of taking it away.

Then he gets down to the matter at hand. "I talked to your doc," he says. He cocks his head as he offers a sympathetic but somehow gloating smile. "She's gonna take you off the Xanax."

His words send a shiver of fear through my body. "But I need it to sleep." It took Anna and me nearly a year to find the perfect medication regimen. I'm afraid to tinker with it just when I'm showing such progress.

I've heard horror stories about withdrawal from benzos. Trouble sleeping. Anxiety. Depression. Intense sweating. Blurred vision. Some people tell me it's worse than going off heroin. Even though I've dabbled in hardcore drugs, I've never been addicted and so never had to experience the journey through hell that is withdrawal. I don't want to go there now.

When I get home, I immediately call Anna and get voicemail. "Dr. Anna Blumenthal is the physician on call. If this is an urgent matter, press one to talk to the doctor immediately. If not, press two to leave a message." I hesitate but end up pressing two.

She calls me back not long after. "I disagree with Hazelden about your medication, but I have to say, you're doing so much better," she tells me. "I can hear it in your voice. I'm really proud of you. I won't let Xanax kick you out of Hazelden." Although I'm still hesitant, I agree to go off the meds, with Anna promising to be available should I need her.

The first night without the Xanax, I have vivid, bizarre nightmares. But luckily it's a one-night thing. Two days later, I can't believe how good I feel. I walk a little taller, proud that I've jettisoned another chemical crutch.

Halfway through the program Tony says, "In the first twenty-eight days, don't do anything drastic. Don't buy a new house. Don't change your job. Don't spend a lot of money." Monica doesn't heed Tony's advice. She cuts ten inches off her hair. And she adopts a Boston terrier puppy, which she names Grace.

Rehab is not a cakewalk for everyone in our group. Paul, a twentysomething culinary student who's joined the group around the same time I have, relapses during his second week, getting stoned one night. He doesn't say anything about it until he gets the results of his latest drop, as if somehow it will go unnoticed. Tony and Paul decide he's a candidate for inpatient rehab, so off he moves into the house, where he'll get extra group time and be obliged to attend a certain number of AA meetings every week.

We don't get to say goodbye to Paul. We all know he's relapsed, and some of the others are shaken, wondering if they'll be next. But not me. I know I'm going to make it. I want it that badly.

I start attending AA meetings myself toward the end of rehab. In the Alcoholics Anonymous program, members are supposed to pick a "higher power greater than ourselves" that will "restore us to sanity." A higher power can be God (which the agnostics among us define as "Group Of Drunks"), nature, or anything of importance to the individual. Seeing as how I don't believe in God, I choose music as my higher power. Music moves me. It makes me feel tingly all over and is its own high. A natural high.

Day 39 of rehab: early March. I'm almost done with my six-week outpatient treatment. My head is clear. My appearance is neat. I've shaved. I was drunk for the better part of five years, and now I'm one month sober. Tony gives us an assignment before we go: Tell our stories to the group.

* * *

I wake up at 7:30 one morning, full of energy, and clean my apartment until it's spotless. A visitor wouldn't recognize this from the apartment of just two months ago. The piles of beer cans are gone, the dishes are all cleaned and stacked neatly in the cabinets and not piled in the sink, the living room is tidy and welcoming. I look around and am pleased by what I see. Then I start writing.

I know that everyone else will be giving an extemporaneous speech, but not me. I write mine down. The story pours out of me. I attack my keyboard and finish the whole piece in two hours. My entire life condensed into thirteen pages.

The suicide attempt. The crack smoking. The hanging out with homeless people. The mania at MTV. The shopping sprees. The hallucinations. The two-inch gash on my forehead. The broken nose. The unprotected sex with Jeffrey. I don't hold anything back. I've no more secrets to hide.

I'm nervous as I take my place before the group of friends who were strangers not so long ago. They've shared as much of their emotions as I have mine, but I've still got a few surprises for them that might change their views of me. I'm having second thoughts about revealing so much. So when I start, it's hesitantly. My former shyness returns as I read the first few words.

"There's a jukebox in my head. It plays songs all day long …"

I'm glad I've begun my essay with music references. It puts me in a comfortable space that allows the words to come more freely. By the time I get to the second page, I can tell people are hanging on every word, so I begin reading faster and faster. It's like a staged reading of a play for me. I'm proud of what I've written.

My nerves begin to buzz again when I reach the section about the drug use. There's no turning back now. "I started smoking crack.

I became friends with the dealers, who were all crack addicts. I would buy a rock and go smoke with them under the overpass on Wabash."

I look around to see if anyone's reactions have changed, if perhaps I've lost a few friends or at least their respect. I catch Monica's gaze and see that she's crying. She mouths, "I love you," as she wipes away the tears, then raises a fist, urging me to stay strong.

I head into the home stretch. "Music sounds great to me now. Better than ever. I can actually *feel* the music instead of listening to it numb. It tingles down my spine. I still listen to music for a couple hours every night. I don't need alcohol anymore. Music gets me high."

At the end, all is quiet. After thirty seconds or so, Tony breaks the silence. "Amazing … amazing."

CHAPTER 11

THE GRATEFUL GROCERY CLERK

2015

Despite being sober three years, I don't feel ready to rejoin the corporate world. My doc wants me to take "baby steps," which makes me feel better. Forty or fifty hours a week with daily pressures seems daunting, even as I fondly remember those late nights meeting deadlines at MTV. And my anxiety and shaky hands limit the kinds of jobs that would be suitable for someone re-entering the workforce. "Baby steps," I repeat to myself. I'll get back there one day.

My parents have talked about getting me on disability, but at the moment my psychiatrist says I am perfectly fit to work as many as thirty hours a week. Some bipolar people, like my high school friend Tara, are on disability because anxiety or rapid-cycling bipolar makes it difficult or even impossible to work.

My parents have been supporting me financially, both during my drinking-and-drugging days and now, three years into sobriety, while I chase my dream of getting published. I need an income to contribute. I also need to get out of the apartment more often.

At this point, any job will do. I desperately want to work at a record store, but even with my background and experience in music, the market is quite competitive.

I manage to score an interview at one of my favorite shops, Reckless Records. The interview lasts five minutes and is more of an informal conversation. We chat music a bit. I send a thank-you card. Two weeks later I'm asked to endure a baptism-by-fire trial day.

The computer system Reckless uses is ancient — Unix, an operating system that hails from the 1970s. The screens are old-school monochrome, green text on black.

And I can't seem to figure out how to work the cash register because of this outmoded operating system. What next? A rotary-dial phone?

The album sleeves are out in the storefront, but all the vinyl and CDs are stored behind the counter, indexed numerically. Wouldn't alphabetical order make more sense? No, that's not how things are done at Reckless.

Because of this inefficiency, it takes me forever to find each record, CD, or DVD, and some customers arrive at the checkout bearing huge stacks of vinyl or CD sleeves. Each record is its own fishing expedition.

My anxiety deepens further when I allow myself to think about how slow I am. My hands tremble violently — most noticeably on the keyboard. It's so bad I ditch my quick touch-typing and decide to type with one finger so that no one sees I have the shakes. I ask my supervisor if I can step outside and make an important call. In a panic, I call my new, Chicago-based doc, who urges me to keep at it. My brain is so fried by the end of the nine-hour day that I'm relying on the other cashiers to take my customers.

I don't get the job. I receive an email saying that they ended up hiring someone with experience inspecting and grading vinyl. I conclude that you have to be a numbers guy to work at Reckless. And I'm a grammar guy; I tinker with words. I don't think I would've taken the job had it been offered anyway. Too fraught.

My sister tells me there might be something at a grocery store where she shops. A few days later I go in for my interview at the Lakeshore East branch of Faziano's, an upscale, Milwaukee-based supermarket chain that also manufactures its own line of food and grocery supplies.

Lakeshore East is a planned community, basically a square with a large park smack dab in the middle and condos surrounding it. Lady Gaga owns a penthouse in the Aqua Building at the top of the 'hood.

"What kind of payment are you expecting?" Matt, the thirtysomething general manager of the store, asks me during an interview.

"Minimum wage," I say. I doubt a job like this offers much more, so I lowball myself. I haven't earned minimum wage since high school. I must sound desperate.

We engage in standard job-interview back-and-forth — why I want to work there, what my best assets are, and so on. He doesn't say, "You're hired." Instead, he rubs his goatee and wonders, "Hmmm … where to put you? Are you a vegetarian?"

I'm not, but I'm not comfortable handling raw meat, so I pass on working in the butcher department. "I used to bag at a grocery store in high school. I could do that again," I say, without thinking first. Big mistake.

"Really?" replies Matt, looking a bit surprised, as if he couldn't conceive of bagging as anyone's first choice. "You want to be a bagger? OK. We'll start you out there and maybe transition you to another job in a different department."

I once was a bagger at Carnival Grocery, a small indie store with only eight aisles, down the street from where I grew up. People would shop for their daily necessities, just what was for dinner that night. So the burden of bagging was light, usually just a bag per customer. Easy-peasy.

Which is why I thought I could handle the job I'd aced in high school. But Faziano's is no Carnival. With my anxiety and bipolar, bagging is now a high-stress endeavor for me. People line up with shopping carts overflowing with groceries that they then unload on the conveyor belt at top speed. Sometimes the groceries fly down so quickly I feel like I'm on a Japanese game show.

When customers want paper bags, we have to double them up. For some reason I can't master the art of the double bag. It's never clean and interlocking when I do it. It's sloppy. Bagging is like an advanced game of Tetris. You have to carefully fit each item in the bag, turning and adjusting to get the maximum number to fit just so, while simultaneously not jostling the items so that they become damaged.

At the same time, the products are flying down the belt and piling up around me like so many Tetris blocks on the screen. But unlike a video game, there is no reset button, no reprieve where I can start over on a slower, less difficult level. There's almost never a pause. I'm the world's most awkward bagger. If I feel I'm slowing down the line even by a few seconds, my anxiety kicks in and I have trouble breathing.

It doesn't take long for me to come to hate Matt. He walks around the store with a pompous smirk on his face, looking dissatisfied. Very, very dissatisfied. When he segues from stocking the shelves one moment to cashiering the next, it's as if he's showing off skills the rest of us lack, even though his are merely minimum-wage skills — and we can, in fact, do them just as well as he can. My bipolar consistently requires stimulation, so I would welcome the opportunity to flit around the store like Matt. But he's the manager. Only he is allowed to take on such diverse responsibilities.

In addition to Matt the Magnificent, I work with a majority of black teenagers and a handful of twentysomethings who already have kids. I can't imagine supporting a family on Faziano's wages. Most of us work part time. (The manager-types work a full forty

119

hours a week and so receive benefits.) Some of them supplement their twenty-five-hour workweek with a second job. They all get food stamps and Medicaid. When I hear their stories, I feel lucky and incredibly grateful to have a family that's supporting me. The added pressure of having to make ends meet would probably cause me to have a mental breakdown. I don't know how I'd react if I had to provide for a family. The thought alone brings on a mild panic attack.

Faziano's employees are required to wear a uniform — white dress shirt, plain black tie, black pants, black dress shoes, and black socks. One morning at my local coffee shop, the woman at the register asks, "What do you do? Are you in *Book of Mormon?*" We have a good laugh when I tell her where I work.

Faziano's is a high-end store. A pianist plays jazz on the weekends. There's an extensive organic salad bar and a hot foods section, offering anything from meatloaf or mac and cheese to steamed broccoli. Also on hand are fresh panini and stone-hearth pizza, a café with gelato and every kind of coffee drink, a chocolate shop, a smoothie bar, and the obligatory upscale bakery. And of course a wine bar.

Getting trashed at the grocery store. Yeah, it's a thing now. Every Saturday and Sunday, there's a mimosa party that lasts all day and gets pretty raucous. Every time a champagne bottle is popped, everyone yells "Mimosa!" kind of like "Opa!" at a Greek restaurant. But instead of flaming cheese, the bartender offers mimosas with freshly squeezed Faziano's orange juice. The chants are a steady reminder that puts drinking on my mind every twenty minutes. Luckily, I was always more of a Bellini guy, so the temptation is muted.

After a couple of weeks of bagging, I'm all tuckered out. I come home from work with my brain destroyed and take naps that are so long they're really like second rounds of sleep. My bipolar brain isn't fit for this work, so I finally speak up about it. "I don't think I'm cut out for bagging," I tell the co–general manager. I get reassigned.

"Lot captain." The title sounds impressive, but rather than helming the *Starship Enterprise*, I'm charged with wrangling shopping carts from the parking lot and bringing them back into the store. I also have to make sure there are plenty of carts on both of Faziano's two levels. When the store is bustling, it's a monumental task, akin to herding cats, except the cats are large, metal, and wheeled. Fortunately, my early-day shift is slow, even when the conveyor belts inside are turning at full speed.

It's so slow that I also get tasked with cleaning the bathrooms every hour. And I'm so bored I do it meticulously. It doesn't matter if I scrubbed that toilet an hour ago; I do it again. After a few weeks, I master the art of bathroom cleaning and receive praise from the store director, Besmir. Cleaning the bathrooms is a much better fit for my bipolar brain. They say bipolar people are likely to notice a tiny speck on the floor but miss the big picture. I'm moving slowly, though, and I actually care about doing a good job, so I don't take the easy route.

As lot captain, I'm also considered to be a "general," meaning I can take on random tasks as needed, like putting out the floor-mats when it rains.

One day I'm tasked with cleaning up a bottle of wine a customer dropped. This one is a Spanish red, Marqués de Cacéres Rioja Gran Reserva. I would recognize that gold-and-burgundy label and serif font anywhere. Fate. I'm a sucker for Spanish reds.

I pick up the large shards of glass and toss them, then grab a mop, bucket, and a yellow WET FLOOR/PISO MOJADO sign from the back room. The smaller bits of glass I'll sweep up after I'm done mopping. The aroma is enticing. I resist the urge to get down on all fours and lick up the spill like a thirsty puppy dog. This is my closest encounter with wine since I've gotten sober. I should have told my supervisor that I was "allergic" to alcohol, which is true. In AA, they talk about alcoholism being "an allergy of the body and an obsession of the mind." I power through it, doing my best to ignore the aisles and aisles of shiny-happy-sexy bottles of wine, liquor, and craft beer as they glisten like a Gustav Klimt painting. The bottles truly are beautiful, even if you're not an alcoholic. I find myself eyeing a bottle of Bombay Sapphire Gin, its azure color as enticing as the Caribbean. And I wasn't even a drinker of hard liquor.

As a music aficionado, I find the worst part of my job to be not the uptight customers or the little brats who throw tantrums at the register when their parents refuse to buy them an overpriced cupcake. No, it's the elevator music the store pipes into every corner and every aisle — even my bathroom sanctuary — that drives me nuts. I have to endure watered-down versions of my favorite songs ad nauseam, and it nearly ruins The Beatles for me.

Since part of my job is to clean the bathrooms every hour, I hear the music loud and clear. The music in the bathroom is louder than it is in the store. So I'm scrubbing toilets to watered-down Frank Sinatra standards. I'm. In. Hell.

I decide to go on a musical crusade and write a letter to the company CEO.

Dear Mr. Faziano,

Everything about Faziano's is unique. The pianist. The cookouts. The wine bar. The stone hearth pizzas. Everything, that is, except the music played in the store. I'm a lot captain at the Faziano's Lakeshore East location in Chicago. I'm also a former producer for MTV News in New York.

I also helped music supervise the Torino Olympics for NBC. That means I picked music that was used on the air for the Games.

I know how to create playlists that capture the essence of a client's brand.

Enclosed please find a demo CD I made of music I would play in the store if I were setting the scene for the Faziano's shopping experience. It includes classic and modern jazz, mild rock, and folk music. There is no hip-hop, rap, or country. This is just a taste of what I can curate for you.

I think playing authentic music in the store would boost team morale as well as keep customers shopping longer.

Please consider using my services. I can create an eighteen-hour music playlist that will enrich the occasion of visiting Faziano's. Faziano's is classy and sophisticated, and its soundtrack should be too.

Sincerely,

Conor Bezane

I never hear back.

Meanwhile, the Muzak machine starts looping the music in short bursts. Every ten minutes we hear The Beatles' "When I'm Sixty-Four." There's nothing we can do about it.

This I can't handle. I absolutely hate "When I'm Sixty-Four." It's one thing to hear an elevator-music version of a song you like — U2's "With or Without You," for example, which sucks as Muzak yet is tolerable — but it's entirely different to hear a song you already find irritable made even more irritating. "When I'm Sixty-Four" is a pockmark on the near-masterpiece that is The Beatles' *Sgt. Pepper's Lonely Heart's Club Band*. It's just a goofy tune not worthy of *Rolling Stone*'s number-one album of all time. And it's coming at me over and over again.

The annoying clarinet trio on the original is even worse on this "digitized" version. Not only does it pop in my head in my waking hours, it haunts me as I try to sleep. This is not the first time I have had rough nights with an earworm in my brain. One time I couldn't get Lady Gaga out of my thoughts as she sang the chorus to "Poker Face" on a loop. My doctor and I upped the dose of my antipsychotic the next day.

After several days, during which I feel like I'm on the brink of becoming manic again, someone fixes the Muzak machine.

Hallelujah! I regain some of my sanity and go about my cart wrangling and toilet scrubbing, contented as if I were running through strawberry fields.

One day I'm so bored I go around asking various co-workers if they need any help. The pricing clerk takes me up on my offer, giving me a stack of sale tags and telling me to find the products and put the stickers on the rails.

Besmir asks what I'm doing. When I tell him, he says, "That's awesome!" with gusto. "Do you have any aspirations at this store, or do you just want to be a lot captain?"

"I've always really enjoyed baked goods, and I'd like to see how they're made," I say.

A couple of hours later, the co–general manager informs me that I have been selected as Ambassador of the Week. I get a twenty-dollar gift card to the store and my picture is hung in the break room. The whole thing is kind of cheesy. But it makes me feel like I'm appreciated.

Matt is responsible for the scheduling. The next day, he comes up to me and says, "Are you sure you wanna work in the bakery? You'll be giving up your cushy hours." It's like he wants me to fail. But finally he gives in.

I start at the bakery in February, just before the Valentine's Day rush and my three-year sobriety anniversary.

The aromas are ethereal. Sometimes the cinnamon-raisin-walnut bread we sell by the pound is fresh out of the oven when I arrive. White chocolate-chip cherry macadamia-nut cookies have a distinctly flavorful essence that nearly makes me drool.

The display case is a spectrum of color. We showcase decadent buttercream chocolate cupcakes, sinful donuts like the maple-bacon long john, rainbow-sprinkled cookies, and everything from tiramisu to Black Forest chocolate cake to fresh-filled-to-order cannoli. I'm clumsy with the cannoli and always make a mess with the pastry bag, but otherwise I feel right at home in the bakery. The pace isn't terribly hectic, I have a true passion for the products, and my coworkers are some of my favorite people in the store.

My eighty-year-old bakery cohort, Donna, greets me every day. She has short-cropped dyed-red hair and loves Faziano's so much she arrives at 3:30 in the morning to fill bagel, cookie, and catering orders, despite the fact she's not on the clock till 6.

"You're my special friend," she says to me one day. When I tell her I'm writing a book, she tells me she's impressed and then talks about the books she reads — mostly Christian nonfiction about miracles and the like. Every time I see her she gives me a big hug. I develop a true fondness for her, as if she were a family member. I wonder what she would think if she knew about my checkered past.

I spend my time waiting on customers and also packaging breads, cookies, and pies while simultaneously trying to avoid Kiki, a gruff old Russian woman who drops in every day demanding her square of chocolate "tuxedo truffle" cake fresh, as in straight out of the freezer. Cutting slices of frozen cake is a drag. Despite Kiki, the job sure beats wrangling carts and cleaning toilets, and I especially look forward to seeing other regular customers.

The bakery is the most cheerful corner of the grocery store. People coming here are friendly and happy. They're treating themselves, so they're typically in a good mood. Leroy shows up daily for his black-olive focaccia muffin. He doesn't need to say a word; I just grab it when I see him coming down the aisle, and he thanks me with a wink.

Then there's George, an elderly man with dementia who arrives in a wheelchair with his wife every afternoon to pick out a donut. I feel bad when we're running low on the donut selection and he doesn't have as wide an array to choose from. His Faziano's bakery visit is clearly the highlight of his day, and I do everything I can to make it as enjoyable as possible.

Samar, our new store director, had started in November. He's Hindu and won't allow Christmas music to be played, so no reprieve from the Muzak. Now that I'm at the bakery, he praises my customer-service skills, saying that I'm always "on it," that I'm "in it to win it," and that I develop good rapport with the customers. Then he decides to try me out in "demo," retail-speak for sampling.

My first duty is to hawk Irish soda bread and Kerry Gold butter in the days leading up to St. Patrick's Day. I set up a table, pull a green plastic tablecloth from the store shelves, and slice up mini pieces of the bread, spreading them with the butter and placing them in little paper cups on a tray.

The product is indeed very good. I offer it to customers. "Would you like to try some Irish soda bread?" I ask probably five hundred times that day. I get rejected four hundred times. As an über-sensitive bipolar soul, I don't deal well with rejection, even if it's something as trivial as soda bread that I didn't even make. I can't help but take it personally.

You would think sampling would be a social job, but it's not. The majority of people walking past my table just offer blank stares or ignore my question as if they can't hear me, like I'm not even there. Most who do take a sample don't say a word and continue their shopping. I'm lucky if I get a smile. We might as well have a machine distributing the samples. It would probably get more attention than I do.

I'm isolated in the middle of the supermarket, seemingly miles from my beloved bakery even though it's just ten feet away. No one to talk to.

Meanwhile, the soda bread is flying off the shelves. I'm a natural, apparently. Either that or the bread is just irresistible. At the end of the day, Samar calls me into his office along with my bakery boss and tells me that I sold three times as much soda bread as the person who did it the day before me.

"This is your new job," Samar tells me. He doesn't ask, he just announces. He also promotes me without giving me a raise, which is against the rules of the United Food and Commercial Workers Union, of which I am a member.

I call the union and they give me some mumbo jumbo about having to "level up," that I should ask for training to become "level two," and that all samplers are at least level two. I know this job is temporary, so I decide not to pursue the matter.

Demo-ing is nerve-wracking. Likely stressful for anyone, it's especially so for my bipolar brain. It's a different kind of stress — one you feel in your whole body, not just your shoulders. A back rub won't do the trick; I would need a full-body massage daily to manage this kind of stress. And I can't afford that. Maybe I should look for a massage-therapist boyfriend on OkCupid.

I also need social stimulation. Someone to talk to. Because of my bipolar brain, I don't do well standing in place with nothing to do for more than a few minutes. My mind starts to wander and race. And after work, the fatigue is worse than if I had put in a normal shift.

But I soldier through. Because what's most important is that being employed at Faziano's proves I can in fact work and that I don't need to be on disability. Granted, I'm doing it only fifteen hours a week, but that's more than a lot of people — including myself — thought I could manage. Faziano's is the only post-college employment experience I've had where I don't absolutely love the work. I always *loved* my writing gigs. At Faziano's, despite days when I feel sick to my stomach with anxiety about going in, I persevere.

CHAPTER 12

THE SOBER LIFE

2017

I'm texting with my friend Skye, who has become my new concert buddy. She never knew me when I was in the throes of addiction and so doesn't really know the extent to which my life has been chaotic and unmanageable.

It's an hour-long back-and-forth text-a-thon. I don't know why we're having this conversation over text and not in person, but that's what's happening. I tell her about the bipolar and all that happened.

At the end of our chat, I write, "Yep, your friend Conor is a little bit crazy."

She texts me back without pause: "No, my friend Conor is stronger than I can even comprehend."

I've never thought about it that way. I've just rolled with the flow. But I am indeed strong, I realize.

I survived a suicide attempt. I evaded crack addiction. I endured the hysterical crying that came with a yearlong depression. I outlived the hallucinations that my life was being broadcast on TV. I even have a scar to show for it all: the two-inch gash on my forehead. The broken nose has healed. I rode out the panic attacks. I'm safe. And I'm prospering.

I'm not moving up on a corporate totem pole as I thought I would when I graduated college. But that's not what I want anymore anyway. What I do want is to write books, and from the friendly confines of my home. I keep plugging away. I've built a solid half-decade of sobriety and stability.

This is the new me. The new me doesn't get drop-dead drunk at every opportunity. The new me tries to write every day, even if it's just a few lines. The new me has planted flowers on the patio. The new me spends money on concert tickets instead of beer. The new me takes out the garbage before it overflows. The new me bakes homemade lasagna for friends. The new me accepts all friend requests, even from strangers. Because there is already enough mistrust and loneliness in the world. The new me is starting to feel like a human being again.

Now I'm sitting in my home office, click-clackety-clacking at my keyboard, reflecting on the past decade.

There's a photo on my office wall of me standing in front of the Brooklyn Bridge wearing my manic purchases — the $1600 suit jacket and $300 pair of sunglasses. It was taken after Mother's Day brunch 2008, before the alcoholic madness. I look good. I'd like to think I look good again now. And people indeed have told me so.

I find it ironic that in sobriety I've developed a beer gut. Or maybe it's just a pre–middle-age potbelly. But I'm working to fix that — seventy-five sit-ups a day.

And brick by brick on TheBipolarAddict.com, I've assembled a community, one that grows daily. I have readers who have become friends, and I offer them advice or comfort, which gives me purpose and helps me cope with the down times. The site and its accompanying Facebook page provide a place where a community can meet and engage. It's very much a "we're all in this together" situation. We who are bipolar have built a fellowship hidden in society. We help each other overcome obstacles. Our community flourishes with compassion and harmony.

To be honest, I am not always a happy camper. I have a dual diagnosis, after all. As I write this, I am crawling out of a deep depression exacerbated by the darkness of winter and lack of sunlight. To top it all off, Trump is president.

But I know it gets better. It always does. It's also better than being stuck in the snake pit of alcoholic lunacy that took over my life. I don't even crave alcohol anymore. In fact, the very smell of it bothers me.

A photographer shot me the other day for a feature in an issue of *BP Hope*, better known as *Bipolar Magazine*. I have become a little bit internet famous through my online presence, albeit with a niche community.

Entering my sixth year of sobriety, I've learned that living the sober life is like hearing your favorite band for the first time every day. Sobriety stays with you forever, but you have to work at it. With the addiction behind me, I feel better. More like myself. I don't stay up all night wasting my time drinking. I don't sleep till 2PM. When I wake up every day, instead of nursing a hangover I drink coffee and watch the morning news. I have wonderful relationships with my family and friends. And nothing could be more fulfilling.

I get to play with my now nine-year-old nephew, which wouldn't be happening if I hadn't chosen the sober path. We play Nintendo together and I make mixtapes for him, teaching him about music. I've taken him to Lollapalooza, where we watched Tegan and Sara, who unfortunately didn't perform their *Lego Movie* hit "Everything Is Awesome." I gave him my old iPod Touch and loaded it with just a bit of music I think he'd like — a mixture of rock, pop, punk, and hip-hop. And I've furthered his arts education by exposing him to avant-garde works like those of Japanese pop artist Takashi Murakami in his recent show of new anime-inspired art. I'm trying to be the cool uncle, rather than the drunkle I once was. And I'd like to think I'm succeeding.

It's still a bit icy with Colleen, my sister. I don't think she understands the severity of my dual diagnosis — and how challenging it is to stay both sober and stable. She exudes the attitude of "on to the next," that I should just "pull myself up by my bootstraps." As if it were that easy.

I also think she resents the fact that I am currently not bringing in any money and that our parents are supporting me. It's clear that she doesn't want to worry about supporting me when my parents pass, which is one reason my parents gave me my inheritance early so I could purchase an apartment — one less financial matter to worry about.

My psychiatrist has changed his mind about my work potential. Based on my anxiety and depression — exhibited at Faziano's and Reckless Records — he believes I should in fact be on disability. And with the help of my high-school friend Tara, I'm applying. But I'm not giving up on work altogether. Even if I'm on disability, I can still have a small income. I continue to have hope that I'll find a job that's more my speed.

I'm hoping that once I'm on disability Colleen's fears will subside and she'll see just how serious my condition is. As kids, we were more than siblings, we were best friends. But we've grown apart over the years. We both have hopes of mending our relation-ship, which is why we're going to therapy together.

I call my mom every couple of days. We have long talks about everything from movies to TV to politics. My mom is my best friend. We have identical taste in movies and have seen some rather edgy ones together — *Pulp Fiction, Requiem for a Dream, Trainspotting* — that we both loved. When she had a stroke a couple of summers ago, I flew to Maui to help around the house and cook low-salt dishes for her new diet, experimenting with mango and lilikoi marinades for fish. And of course I made mixtapes for her, an upbeat, dance-y one for physical therapy and one for relaxation.

I also enjoy making mixtapes for my dad. I curated a Greatest Hits of the '60s disc and a collection of Dixieland jazz, his favorite style. Since he's a fellow writer, I'm constantly bouncing ideas off him. He is one of the most talented writers I've ever read (biased as I may be). We also have something else in common: Dad was recently diagnosed with bipolar II disorder. He's always been a quirky guy to begin with — an absentminded-professor type — so the diagnosis explains a lot. We're the oddballs in the family. In a good way.

I'm also dating again. That part's been a challenge since I moved to Chicago's Andersonville. Even though it's a very gay neighborhood, everyone seems not only coupled up but also settled down. I've gotten over my initial fears about putting myself out there, though, which feels like a major milestone.

Everyone around me is beyond supportive. And therapy is going swimmingly. I still need therapy to manage my moods, which ebb and flow. But thankfully, my moods now are less like a thrill-ride roller coaster than a spin in the teacups. My meds are tweaked every now and then.

I know I will never drink again. I don't want to. The very thought repulses me, the remembered taste too potent and vile. I'll take a nicotine buzz over a beer buzz anytime. But I've quit smoking. Cigarettes were the one vice I allowed myself. I still dream about drinking — but those are nightmares now.

Today I am grateful for music, my greatest coping mechanism. Listening to live music is like attending church. I worship at the altar of Apollo, the god of music. My stomping grounds are festivals like Lollapalooza, Pitchfork, and Riot Fest, or regular shows at the Metro and the Riviera — but no longer the Fireside Bowl (which is a bona fide bowling alley once again).

Above all, I'm grateful for my family, friends, and my dual-recovery community. If we can stay sober together, we can survive together. If we can pat each other on the back for our milestones, if we can take our meds as prescribed, if we can avoid triggers, if we can notice the beauty in the world, if we can advocate for peace and love and acceptance, if we can laugh together, cry together, rewrite our lives together, then we can come alive together. With love, luck, and laughter, we will thrive together.

Five years down, and a lifetime to go. Bring it on!

PART II
THE ECCENTRICS

We are punks. We are poets.
Musicians and artists. Professionals and intellectuals.
We are drunk. High. Manic. Depressed. We almost died.
And now we are stable and sober.

CHAPTER 13

THE CON ARTIST

*"How I didn't die so many hundreds upon hundreds
of times is beyond my wildest imagination."*

The con goes like this: Print fake business cards. Shower and shave at the homeless shelter. Apply makeup to disguise dark circles. Dress in a freshly dry-cleaned suit. Hit downtown.

"I was a hundred-dollar-an-hour con artist," says Jason of the years during which he was addicted to crack and heroin. He recites the one-minute spiel he used on his marks back in the day: "I'm the vice president of Chase Bank. I just flew in from Boston. I had an early-morning powwow at the Chicago Board of Options Exchange and my Range Rover got towed. My wallet was in my laptop case on the backseat. Can you help?"

He'd solicit money from passersby with the promise that he'd mail them a check later. And it worked. Complete strangers shelled out upward of 100 bucks a pop.

Jason attributes his success, as both a con artist and salesman, to the enthusiasm fueled by his hypomania. "When I can harness and use it effectively," he explains, "I get above-average results in anything I do." For Jason, mania is his superpower.

Over the course of five years, Jason had a nasty, multi-thousand-dollar crack cocaine and heroin habit. The con fed that habit.

In the rooms of AA, people often say it's not just a drinking problem, it's a thinking problem. Jason's thinking problem began early. "I started running from things," he says of his youth. "I was full of anger and rage and fear and lust and dysfunction and dishonesty. That was who I was — unbalanced and erratic."

Growing up, Jason never lived in one place for very long. His family, plagued with money troubles, moved around Chicago and its suburbs. By the time he graduated, he'd attended twelve different schools.

To add to the instability, his parents were alcoholics and his dad would get violent when he drank. Jason remembers one time when his father pulled him out of bed and started beating him. "He kicked me with his pointed boots in my rectum so hard that I thought I was going to die."

At holiday gatherings, the entire family was so drunk that Jason had no trouble sneaking enough sips to get buzzed himself.

Despite the dysfunctional home life, he managed to enjoy some childhood pleasures, such as playing baseball and football from sunrise to sundown. Later, in high school, he joined the wrestling team and got good grades, even though he had trouble "quieting the mind" or even reading for more than twenty minutes at a time. He eventually learned he had attention deficit hyperactivity disorder, ADHD.

Jason moved out of the house when he was seventeen and crashed with his brother. That's when the substance abuse that had lain dormant in his DNA was awakened. He started drinking alcoholically, smoking pot, and doing cocaine. Not more than a couple of years after high school, his cocaine addiction was full blown.

After fighting with his brother over the cleanliness of the apartment they shared, Jason moved back in with his parents.

In spite of his chronic womanizing at the time, Jason got engaged, but he soon learned his fiancée was cheating on him and so called it off. He next started a relationship with a woman thirteen years his senior who hung around with a group of derelicts. The coke use intensified. "I'd be pulling all-nighters and two-dayers," he says, all while working as a computer salesman in downtown Chicago for a period of three years. After a verbal argument with a coworker almost turned physical, Jason was let go from his job.

Jason had dropped out of junior college after one semester. His career was sporadic and his resume had huge holes.

He started doing some catalogue modeling. At one point his agency got him an audition for a Miller Lite commercial. He was all set to do it but missed the audition because he was too stoned to get there. Other times he'd be booked for runway shows and not show up because he was too hungover.

Next came a flurry of jobs. From branch manager to inventory manager to operations manager to sales manager to recruiting, he was constantly getting fired from whatever gig he managed to land. Payday would come and he'd go on five-day coke benders. Sometimes he took server or bartender jobs at pricy restaurants. With nightly tips, every day was payday.

When Jason got his bipolar diagnosis in the late '90s, he went on lithium as well as so many other medications that he lost count. "I never stayed sober long enough for them to have any effect," he admits.

Powder. Powder. Powder. Crack. Powder. Powder. Powder. Crack. That became his routine. It was never social. His paranoia — a hallmark of bipolar — kept him alone in a room with the door locked.

Jason would climb on top of a dumpster in an alley near Rush Street, in one of Chicago's nightlife districts, and make his way through the window of a transvestite prostitute's room. She would go out and buy crack with Jason's money and they'd smoke it together in the roach-and-rat-infested hotel room.

Jason doesn't recall any particular manic episodes. Since he is bipolar II, he was constantly hypomanic, a lesser degree of mania without hallucinations and psychosis.

"I talk fast. I'm truly extroverted," he says. "I can talk so fast at times that I overwhelm people. It's just the way my brain flies."

And throughout our interview, Jason indeed talks at turbo speed and jumps all over the place in the chronology of his life.

After his stint getting high with the transvestite prostitute, Jason jumped in and out of rehabs, staying sober for up to three months at a time before relapsing and starting all over again. He rattles off the names of rehabs the way someone else would European vacation destinations. Rehab was like a cleansing of the body he engaged in every few months before picking back up again. He just couldn't shake the addiction, so needing to feed it, he cooked up another scheme — this one involving a fake wife.

Starving for cash to feed his habit, Jason concocted a con to steal from cab drivers. After faking a call with a made-up wife, during which he'd pretend to argue about running late and having no time to stop for cash, he'd ask the cabbie to break a hundred. When the driver handed over the cash, Jason would grab it and run. This time he wasn't as lucky as when he'd run his towed–Range Rover con: He got caught and slapped with his first felony. On another occasion, what should have been a misdemeanor was upgraded to a felony because of Jason's prior arrest for possession.

In between scamming taxis, he resorted to dumpster diving for food. His scavenging sometimes yielded such treasures as silk ties and Hugo Boss suits.

If he didn't have the money to buy drugs, he suffered terribly. His heroin habit's hold was so intense that when his system began to run low on the drug, he'd have to go to the emergency room for morphine, which would alleviate the withdrawal symptoms for half a day. If they gave him Vicodin for the pain, he'd pop the full twenty-two pills in one sitting. Even such a large dose, likely lethal for anyone else, had little effect on his wildly inflated tolerance for narcotics.

During his withdrawal, his nose would run, he'd sneeze constantly, his bowels would churn, and he'd start gagging on bile. "It's like having the worst stomach flu in your whole body times one hundred," he says. "That's literally how you feel when you're dopesick."

Jason lived in the ghetto in an abandoned building. Even the heroin-addicted prostitutes wouldn't live in the rat-infested place he occupied.

"Everybody knew me, and I knew everybody," he says. He was the only white guy in the neighborhood. "The police would look at me and for some reason just keep going. For years they never stopped me."

But then one night they did.

It happened when he was so desperate, he'd just stolen heroin and raw crack-cocaine from his drug dealer, who had viewed him as a trusted client and never suspected Jason would betray him. But Jason was broke and he needed his fix. He bolted.

An undercover Crown Victoria pulled up and three drug-enforcement tactical officers emerged, yelling, "Stop, crackhead!" He ditched both baggies, intending to return for them later. After the cops searched him and said he could go, they noticed the baggies and summoned Jason back to the car. The police wanted to put a wire on Jason and have him rat out the dealers in the neighborhood.

He wouldn't do it, so they took him to jail.

"Before you can go to County, you go to lockup," Jason explains. "And County is horrific, but man, it's terrible in lockup. I mean, it's a metal slab, it's ice freezing cold, and you're staring at a brick wall and you're just lying there on this metal slab just detoxing," Jason recounts. "I went to the detox and threw up, like, seventeen times within the first day. Every hour I was gagging yellow bile, but they kept yelling, 'Get cleaned up!' My body was just shutting down, so I went through a horrible, horrible detox. And I stayed there like twenty-seven, twenty-eight days."

Then he went to county jail for three and a half months.

"I really believe that God made sure that I was arrested," Jason says. Detoxing in jail was hell. For more than a month he hardly slept, catching five minutes here and there throughout the day until anxiety forced him wide awake. The withdrawal was so severe he couldn't control his bodily functions. He'd lie in a pile of his own excretions, puking, gagging, and unable to sleep to escape the horror of it all.

It took him one full year of sobriety to be able to sleep six hours straight.

After Jason got probation and sobered up, his hypersensitivity, irritability, and lack of concentration intensified. But somehow he pulled himself together enough to hold down a job he managed to get at a mortgage company as a senior consultant, making large commissions.

* * *

Today, after more than a dozen stints in rehab or detox and three jail sentences, Jason has found religion. The prison's chaplain gave him a Bible, and Jason started attending church when he was released. He is now engaged to Sofia, who has not only never done a drug but has never even been drunk or smoked a cigarette. He describes his fiancée as spiritually disciplined and committed to God.

When they first started seeing each other, Jason was still an active addict. He would never use in front of her, but when she went to her parents' house for a few days, he would binge. Jason was very good at hiding his addictions.

He was still living in a halfway house when he decided he was ready to propose to Sofia. He told the house manager, "I'm going to give her this ring, so I might not be home tonight." To which the house manager replied, "Go give her that rock, don't smoke one." But Jason went straight to the projects and smoked all night, the $8000 ring in his pocket.

After he got into the routine of reading his Bible and going to church, he finally mustered the energy to get sober and did so on May 3, 2011. He attributes his sobriety to God and Alcoholics Anonymous.

At the time of his interview, Jason rented a swanky condo overlooking the lake on the North Side of Chicago. He works in sales for a private yacht charter company in Chicago. He's about to break the company record in sales.

"I was blessed to be able to rent this condo," Jason says. "I keep a savings account and pay my bills on time."

Now Jason goes to a private AA meeting at a friend's house, where they each share what's going on in their lives while eating a home-cooked meal. He also goes to a total of four AA meetings a week. He looks back on his drug-fueled years and is thankful for having made it through. "How I didn't die so many hundreds upon hundreds of times is beyond my wildest imagination," he says.

He describes his current life as good and functional but knows there will be difficult times, particularly since he has chosen to not take medication for his bipolar. "I'm going to have moments of depression. I'm going to have moments of anxiety. I'm going to have moments of fear, resentment, or rage that I can't get rid of." He credits Alcoholics Anonymous with providing him with the structure to make it through those dark times. And, he adds, "My solution is always God. And it will always be God."

The Promises outlined in *Alcoholics Anonymous* have come to fruition for Jason as of a couple years ago. They include "[knowing] a new freedom and a new happiness," knowing peace, the disappearance of "the feeling of uselessness and self-pity" as well as the "fear of people and economic insecurity." But, most of all, the book promises that "[w]e will suddenly realize that God is doing for us what we can't do for ourselves." He, Sofia, and their new baby girl are as happy as a family can be.

And Jason always makes sure to generously tip his cab driver.

CHAPTER 14

THE ACTRESS

"Daddy, I wanna come home."

Kelly is often buried in her moleskin notebook, jotting her latest travails. She has long red hair and dresses colorfully — a lot of down-to-the-floor skirts. Her choice of eye shadow may reflect her moods: dark when she's feeling gloomy and colorful when she's cheerful.

Her life reads like a compendium of yin and yang references: crystal meth addict. Valedictorian. Nervous breakdowns. D.A.R.E. award winner. Fluent in French. Hallucinogens. Acting. Anorexia. Suicide attempt. Dual Recovery Anonymous.

Kelly was a late bloomer. She hated marijuana and alcohol in high school and didn't become addicted to drugs until college, when cocaine became her drug of choice.

Kelly was raised in Park Forest, Illinois, a southwest suburb of Chicago. The daughter of a criminal defense attorney and a travel agent, she came from a loving and stable family. Her parents are even still married. She was a perfectionist and an overachiever, excelling in creative pursuits but socially awkward.

As early as first grade, she showed creative promise. Her teacher would use her art projects as examples for the rest of the class. Around that same time she began taking French, for which she quickly developed a passion that would follow her through life, thanks in part to a language-immersion camp in northern Minnesota that she attended for several summers. When she found her poetic calling, her work was published in an amateur anthology for youth. She even dabbled in an array of sports, mostly at her mother's urging.

While still in grade school, Kelly became involved in D.A.R.E. (Drug Abuse Resistance Education), where she won two medals for her writing. For her award-winning skit, she even got permission to use real beer bottles to stage an authentic party scene in which an attendee overdoses.

In sixth grade, Kelly and three friends dressed up as the Spice Girls for Halloween. Kelly as Baby Spice wore an extremely short, tight skirt. Her older sister bought her a bottle of peach schnapps for the occasion. She and her friends got wasted.

The summer before eighth grade, Kelly was hit by a van and flew ten feet, fracturing her skull. The doctors told her she should have died. Terrible nightmares followed, so she went to a therapist, who diagnosed her with PTSD.

Looking back, Kelly now realizes she was depressed throughout her formative years. Her success and sunny disposition masked the truth from her parents, who attributed her occasional psychological slumps to stress and overextending herself.

It all caught up with her during her sophomore year of high school, when she had a nervous breakdown. The stress of acting in a play and deadlines for three papers pushed her over the edge. Against Kelly's wishes, her mom took her on a vacation to "relax."

"What kind of fifteen-year-old is furious to be missing high school to go on a Caribbean cruise?" Kelly asks. "I was. I had all this work to do. I would get depressed about that. I was fighting the relaxation of it."

Back at school, Kelly attended the requisite keggers but says she was never really attracted to drinking, particularly because her parents allowed her the occasional glass of wine at dinner. Aside from the one time she tried pot (she felt ill after one hit), she never drank or did drugs at parties, choosing instead to read in a bathtub while her classmates got trashed downstairs. One time, when her boyfriend found her curled up in the cool porcelain, he grew angry and conveyed his embarrassment. She replied by calling his friends lame and condemning the popular girls for downplaying their intelligence.

Kelly couldn't wait to go off to college. She chose UCLA, where she double-majored in French and acting. Once on campus, she finally felt able to breathe and be herself. She reveled in the intellectual atmosphere and enjoyed engaging in philosophical and political conversations, even outside of class.

But drugs sucked her in almost immediately upon meeting Caryn, who became a close friend, and Kyle, a crystal-meth addict. Although they weren't part of her circle of drama friends, they still had the intellectual cachet that drew Kelly to them. "They were like, 'Here, do you wanna try cocaine?' I was like, "Sure, let's all do cocaine. Let's do cocaine all night!" It became a regular part of her college life.

"I was invincible," she says, possibly explaining a manifestation of mania. "It was like, *This is fun and they're doing it and they're fine and they say it's cool, so it's cool.*"

College brought an amazing mix of great times — and down times. She remembers her first couple of years of acting school as a form of group therapy.

Much later, when Kelly's mom found out she had been doing drugs in college, she arrived for a visit one day wearing both of those D.A.R.E. medals. "She was like, 'I really think you should give these back,'" Kelly says.

Kelly had body-image issues, and her classmates at UCLA were all skinny and obsessed with their health. Anorexia soon kicked in. Kelly would walk miles and miles every day and stopped eating. She lost fifteen pounds. No one at UCLA knew her old self, so there was no one to notice the changes.

One afternoon she bragged to Caryn, also anorexic, that she hadn't eaten for three days. Caryn jumped at the chance to take it to the next level. "She was like, 'I'm gonna make us cookies with ipecac, and then we're gonna vomit,'" Kelly recalls, seeing this in retrospect as a hypomanic incident.

Soon after, Kelly started self-injuring — hitting herself or pulling at her hair. She convinced herself that punching was normal; cutting was what crazy people did. When people asked about her bruises, she would say they were from stage combat.

As the depression deepened, her hygiene worsened. At one point she didn't wash her hair for two weeks. Her weight had also plummeted to barely 100 pounds. She remembers dressing up for a party and wearing a "super sexy" dress that felt like it was falling off her.

She and her friend Kyle tried hallucinogens. They would eat magic mushrooms and ride the elevator for hours, thinking it the most fascinating activity in the world. On these mushroom trips, Kelly perceived that everyone was saying the most profound, enchanting things. One time, she decided to grab her moleskin notebook to document the moment. As soon as everyone had come down, Kelly couldn't wait to show everyone her writing.

"This is gonna be fucking amazing!" she told them. But when she opened the notebook, it was blank. She'd never actually written anything while high, even though she remembered doing so. The sole scrawl in the notebook was the word "prettyyyyyyy," with the Y duplicated for pages and pages.

Senior year, Kelly accidentally tried crystal meth for the first time when she thought she was snorting a line of cocaine. "I would set these parameters for myself," she says. "*I'll do coke but not crystal. I classified drugs as either a party drug or a white-trash drug.*" In other words, cocaine was classy; meth was not. It was also around this time that her self-harming graduated to cutting.

When she started dating Freddie, a dancer and drug dealer, coke and pot became even more accessible. She began living in a house with addicted creatives, in what she describes as a *Twilight Zone* cocaine nightmare. She relished being productive and creative, which was the opposite of living in a house of people on acid.

One night, The Beatles' *Abbey Road* ended up on repeat until dawn. When the track "Here Comes the Sun" came on, Kelly woke to find everyone lying around still cracked out. She thought, "I have to get the fuck outta here."

Compared with Freddie, Kelly was able to moderate her cocaine use. "An eightball [3.5 grams] would last me a couple weeks," she says. "If Freddie had an eightball, it would be gone the next day."

The couple would stay up all night eating citrus fruit and reading plays to each other. Freddie's apartment was always a wreck, with the dishes stacked high. It was a rude awakening when Kelly realized she needed a line just to wash them up. She was still getting straight A's despite the addictive behavior.

Then Kelly auditioned for the role of a speed addict in an Adam Rapp play. Even after being coked out for days, she did a line in the car before heading in to try out.

And she nailed it. But there was one — very ironic — problem.

The director pulled her aside and, after raving about her audition, told her she didn't look the part. "You have to look gaunt, and there's only so much we can do with makeup," he told her. "You're perfect for this, but you don't *look* like a drug addict. It's not believable."

Although she didn't get the role, Kelly found success in another play, *Alice Sit-by-the-Fire*, by J.M. Barrie. The play brought Kelly out of a deep depression. It received good reviews and ended up a smash, selling out shows for six months. While she was acting, she didn't use cocaine or other drugs because she felt they robbed her of emotion. She even stopped her antidepressants because she didn't want to risk feeling like a zombie and hindering her acting. "I'd rather be fall-down depressed than not have any feelings," she says. She admits she wasn't taking her mental health or her therapy seriously.

When the play's run ended, Kelly fell back into old habits but also resumed taking her antidepressants. She put on weight and continued self-harming. She even began cheating on Freddie with Michael, a fellow actor she says made her feel as if they "were living in a French novel." When they had sex, she would say, "I don't want you rubbing up on my leg. I have cuts on my leg with Band-Aids.'"

She began to experience symptoms of obsessive-compulsive disorder, such as needing to have the same number of cuts on each leg. "A lot of self-injurers are really obsessed with the tools they use. It's all about the knife, or it's all about the scissors," she says, thinking back. "With me, it was all about the Band-Aids and the antiseptic." She savored the scent of each as she applied them to her self-inflicted cuts. "I'd buy forty dollars' worth of Band-Aids and think that was OK."

After another nervous breakdown, Freddie broke up with her. Her depression deepened. "I tend to take to the floor, even sleeping on it, when I'm really low," she says. "I couldn't even make it to the bed."

She went home for a couple of weeks for spring break to visit her parents, who immediately suspected something was wrong. Although she convinced them she was fine, she didn't leave the house for a week. And there was more self-injuring — evidenced by blood all over her clothes. Her parents knew she wasn't OK but remained in denial, believing their beloved daughter would never do such things.

Back in LA, Kelly became suicidal. "I was like, 'Oh my God, if I die here, my dad's gonna have to get on a plane and come get my body,'" she says. "I've always thought that suicide is incredibly selfish, but I'm so attracted to it." It was her dog, Bowie — named after David Bowie — that kept her alive. She didn't want him to starve to death.

One night in 2009, Kelly was desperate. She called her dad at 3 in the morning and told him she wanted to come home. He heard the pain and suffering in her voice when she confessed that she'd been lying about being well and that she was actually a hardcore addict. She also finally admitted she'd been self-injuring.

Her dad immediately booked her a ticket home. She brought only her purse and her dog. After six months, Kelly flew back to LA to close up the apartment her parents had continued to pay for and to put some stuff in storage and bring the rest back to Chicago. During her time home, she hadn't been doing drugs because she didn't know how to get them in the suburbs.

Then, another setback. Kelly learned she had a brain tumor. It was microscopic, but she got sick often and her body thought she was pregnant, which caused her to gain a lot of weight. The prognosis, however, was good: She didn't need surgery, and medicine could manage it.

Mania returned. "I would stay up all night. I was collecting nail polishes. I had over two hundred bottles at the time," Kelly says. She made extremely detailed lists and organized them by color.

After about six months, Kelly moved into a penthouse in the city and met Ryan, a crystal-meth addict. When she went over to Ryan's, she started snorting and smoking crystal meth every day. She was instantly addicted and started trading her Xanax anti-anxiety meds for crystal.

Meth makes you paranoid. When Kelly was on crystal, the paranoia spiked dramatically and sometimes manifested itself as hypergraphia, a compulsive need to write or draw. Either manic, high, or both, she began writing down license plate numbers — hundreds of them — in her trusty notebook.

The day before she got sober, Kelly attempted suicide. She was still doing crystal every day.

She developed auditory hallucinations brought on by the meth. It was her boyfriend's voice. She thought Ryan had bugged her ear. She also thought he was cheating on her.

Kelly's parents loved Ryan because he had a steady job with a six-figure salary. They thought their daughter was merely ill, that she was overdoing it with Ryan. They joked, "You're so in love you're up all night."

She was on medication for depression but wasn't taking mood stabilizers, which probably accounted for the fact she was manic much of the time. Plus, she was always high. With continued meth use, the paranoia intensified, as did the voices. She could hear Ryan whispering in her ear, telling her "they" had already killed her parents and that now "they're gonna kill you. You have to get out now."

She ran barefoot down the forty-five flights of stairs of her high-rise, wearing only a T-shirt, no bra, and sweatpants. When she told the doorman about the voices, he called the police, who then called her dad.

Her father attempted to calm her down. "I'm coming to get you," he said. "You're OK, Mom and I are OK. I'll be there as soon as I can." Then her dad called Ryan, who fessed up about the meth.

Kelly had ingested crystal meth. You can snort crystal meth, you can smoke crystal meth, but you definitely can't eat crystal meth. Kelly knew this but was determined to end it all.

She ended up in the ER. When her parents asked what she had taken, Kelly told them Xanax. But her father pressed and demanded she show them the baggie. There was still meth in it.

In the ICU, she was still convinced the "bad people" were coming to kill her family. She spent a week in the psych ward and detoxed. That's when Kelly got her bipolar diagnosis.

Her dad had had it. "I will not fight you, you're not going back to the hospital," he said. "You're going to jail if you relapse."

Out of the hospital, Kelly started using with Ryan again. She was still paranoid, believing there were soldiers with night-vision goggles watching their every move. She also recommenced self-injuring, now with an X-Acto knife. She slit both of her wrists in the bathroom at her parents' house. Her dad came in and saw her on the floor and smacked her.

That's when she went into a new program, one for those with a dual diagnosis, which she credits for her finally finding sobriety. She could relate better to the other rehab patients and enjoyed the camaraderie she experienced in treatment.

"I was starting to realize that it didn't have to hurt so bad. And I thought I had enough of the traumas under my belt to have an emotional life that I could pull from in my acting," Kelly reflects. "I really want to write about being in these hospital situations, all these crazy stories I keep finding myself in among these truly psychotic people."

But a year into her sobriety and newfound life, Kelly wasn't feeling as hopeful. She thought she might return to acting one day but had become dead-set on becoming an addiction counselor. She is currently taking social work classes online through the University of Southern California.

It's been rough.

"I bit off way more than I could chew," she says of her using and self-injury days. "And I was just bouncing off the walls. I couldn't sleep. I couldn't focus. Racing thoughts. All I wanted was to use in order to calm that down or to balance myself out."

She didn't use and bounced back, celebrating her one-year anniversary sober in February 2014.

But she still feels unfulfilled.

She apologizes that there is no happy ending to this story.

"There's still too much pain in my life daily," she says. "I'm fundamentally a really sad person. I've had too many things that haunt me. I don't have hope — and not being creative really makes me so fundamentally miserable that it's hard to look forward to tomorrow.

"What I really need to do is reconnect to my art and to acting," she explains. "Without them, I don't have a soul."

CHAPTER 15

THE JET-SETTER

*"I don't feel the need right now to use or drink
or spend money or have sex."*

SFO airport. 2005. High on ketamine. Manic. He was wearing sunglasses and a crimson bathrobe with nothing on underneath. Armed with $20,000 in his pockets, he was determined to fly to South America.

"I was trying to buy a first-class one-way ticket to Buenos Aires with no luggage," says Ethan, a thirtysomething Renaissance man with all the trappings of a Brooklyn hipster and who has bounced around the world. "I was waving around what I thought was my passport. Turns out it was a press pass from college."

Ethan never made it to Argentina that day. Instead, the police took him to a psych ward. Rehab followed.

* * *

Ethan was born in 1978 in Lincoln Park, a tree-lined neighborhood filled with young families on the North Side of Chicago. Excelling at math as a boy, he attended Francis W. Parker, a pricy private school. His early youth was dominated by violin lessons, chess tournaments, and other pursuits geared to high achievers. Summers he would go on elaborate vacations with his family — to Bologna, Italy, where his parents owned a house, and his aunt's place on Martha's Vineyard.

In fourth grade, when it became apparent that Ethan was a prodigy, he was sent by his parents, both college professors, to boarding school at the elite Phillips Exeter Academy in New Hampshire, whose alumni include Gore Vidal, John Irving, and Mark Zuckerberg.

High school at Exeter was extremely competitive. Students studied rigorously, vying to get into the best colleges. Ethan had an edge over his classmates because he could stay up for days due to what he later realized were manic episodes.

In his free time, he went apple picking with friends, listened to Nirvana, and had a crush on Kurt Cobain.

During a depression he suffered sophomore year, he saw a psychiatrist, who diagnosed him with bipolar and put him on lithium and Prozac. The pills worked — while he was on them. Because of the stigma around taking psychiatric drugs, once Ethan was feeling better he ditched the medication, convinced he no longer needed it.

Ethan came out while still at Exeter, but it didn't define him. "Long before I was the gay kid, I was the smart kid," he brags. "I just kind of announced it one day. Everyone was very yawningly liberal about it."

As a teenager, Ethan had tasted a little bit of wine and champagne with his parents. The first time he drank the hard stuff was at an Exeter party, where he had two vodka tonics.

"Some people say they had one sip of something and then suddenly they had to drink a whole gallon," Ethan says. "For me, it was a habit that developed in its own time, until in college in the late '90s I started getting fucked up on a regular basis. And I grew to love that habit."

Upon acceptance to Harvard in 1996, he became a physics major but ended up switching to Italian literature — a nod to his family's numerous vacations in Bologna — and took classes in foreign languages, philosophy, and English. He found a drinking buddy in Julia, a fellow Harvard student who was also an alcoholic. They had dinner one night at Casablanca, a Mediterranean restaurant on Harvard Square.

"We had crème brûlée and Bombay Sapphire martinis one night," Ethan says. "We had such a good time we decided we'd go every night. We'd drink four or five giant gin martinis. That always got me wasted."

Ethan would continue to drink every night for the next seven years, and along the way he also picked up a cocaine habit.

In the summer of 1997, before his sophomore year, he landed a gig as the editor of the travel guide *Let's Go Italy* and got his own apartment in Cambridge. There were some older guys at the *Let's Go* office who worked twelve-hour days and partied hard afterward.

Ethan started going to gay clubs with his co-workers and would stay out all night drinking scotch and snorting cocaine with his buddy Armand, who called him Baby Ethan. Manic and hypersexual at this point, Ethan indulged in frequent one-night stands that always involved bingeing on drugs.

"I rolled into my sophomore year of college with a very nasty cocaine habit," he says. "I was doing a gram or two a day for a while. I probably wasn't spending more than a few hundred dollars a week. It was little enough that I wasn't noticing it."

By the end of sophomore year, the drug use had escalated. Ethan tried ketamine and ecstasy. He smoked crack, snorted heroin, dabbled in hallucinogens like acid, mushrooms, mescaline, and salvia, an herb that is still legal but listed as a "drug of concern" by the Drug Enforcement Administration. Ethan viewed the hallucinogens much like hippies did in the '60s — as a means to "turn on, tune in, and drop out," in the words of counterculture guru Timothy Leary. He and Carl, a Harvard Medical School professor, would hole up in fancy hotels and go on drug sprees.

Regarding his coworkers, Ethan says, "These people involved with this were so smart. It did not make abusing drugs seem sordid; it made it seem glamorous — very, very glamorous."

Along the way, Ethan had accumulated quite the glassware collection—sixty champagne flutes, ninety wine glasses, and forty cocktail tumblers, all purchased for a single party. One night he dropped one of the cocktail glasses, slipped, and slit his wrist on the glass, passing out in the process. He was saved from bleeding out because his arm miraculously ended up propped on a book that happened to be on the floor.

But he realized things were getting out of hand, so he decided to take a year off school and move to New York's East Village to "get my head screwed on straight." It was the worst possible destination. He lived at Orchard and Houston, in the heart of the city's hipster nightlife scene at the time. There, it was even easier than in Cambridge to get drunk, do coke, and take home a different guy every night.

One of his one-night stands introduced him to Elena, also an alcoholic and coke addict. She and Ethan hit it off and became roommates. He went back on his bipolar meds but, playing his own doctor, didn't take antipsychotics. Instead, he used alcohol to balance himself out. And returned to Harvard to finish up.

After graduating, he and Elena moved to London, where they worked on a documentary about how Elena's grandmother had been involved in a bank robbery in Bucharest in the late '50s. When the film was finished, Elena went to Indonesia to help some friends with another cinematic project. Ethan, alone in London, started shooting heroin. He was hooked from the very beginning.

"Heroin is the removal of feeling. It takes everything away, and then you are in a vacuum, essentially. Cocaine is just the feeling of *things are happening*," he says, snapping his fingers. "And heroin is the basic feeling of *nothing is happening*. It just felt like peace."

Soon, speedballs — a mix of heroin and cocaine — became his drug of choice. "You're always sort of chasing this feeling of everything being OK and everything also happening at the same time," Ethan says. "And you get it once in a while, but obviously your brain just starts on this endless journey of chasing it."

The last days in London involved drinking alone in his apartment, doing lines, and guzzling whiskey and wine. After running into a former Harvard classmate, Bill, at a party, the two began dating and soon moved to Paris. They settled in with Ethan's friend Veronika, who lived in the Ritz Carlton apartments and hung out mostly with American ex-pats. They often had sex in the public bathroom at the Ritz, until they were politely asked not to.

Ethan saw his time in Paris as "doing nothing," which made him fidgety and uncomfortable, so after six months it was on to the next spot. He and Bill rented an apartment in Vatican City.

"We were doing this young bohemian thing, sloshing around, pretending were in a Henry James novel," Ethan recalls. His family vacations and undergrad classes made him far more comfortable speaking Italian than French, so his nerves were calmed in the new atmosphere. Traveling around so much also meant he wasn't using drugs, since he didn't have a steady dealer. But he was still drinking heavily.

The mania returned. Ethan was now spending vast amounts of money, mostly on clothes. After Italy, he and Bill moved back to

Massachusetts, for lack of a better plan, before finally breaking off their relationship altogether. Single again, Ethan flew to Berlin to live with a friend who owned an art gallery and needed a business partner.

"Here I am in Berlin, a new fun city for me to misbehave in," he remembers. "I was having tons and tons of bathhouse sex. If you do a lot of speed, you end up having sex."

Ethan then moved to San Francisco, which is when he had the incident at SFO. But the rehab that followed didn't stick. Not long after, in September 2011, he moved back to Chicago, where he checked in at Hazelden Betty Ford. Another setback: He tested positive for HIV.

The HIV diagnosis was a wake-up call. Shaken, Ethan vowed to lay off the sauce and junk. This time it took. Today Ethan is in good health and his doctor has not yet put him on any HIV drugs.

He is also sober and complying with his meds. He's been accepted to a graduate literature program at Yale and plans to teach someday. "I am really good at going to school," he says. "I don't know what else I would do with myself."

He feels good — naturally high.

"I'm better than I've been in living memory," Ethan marvels. "I can breathe. I feel stable. I'm not haunted by compulsions every moment. I don't feel the need right now to use or drink or spend money or have sex."

To date, Ethan has spent well over $100,000 on treatment at Hazelden. His psychiatrists have encouraged him to see the addiction, bipolar disorder, and HIV as a single, ongoing battle.

"My addiction is far too deadly," Ethan says. "It's deadly and crazy. My addiction definitely wants to kill me.

"Right now I know one thing: There is something that's killing me a lot faster than HIV, and that's my addiction. I don't have the luxury to freak out about it. The reality is I'm OK. And I'm calm enough that I can sit with myself now and just be."

CHAPTER 16

THE CLARINET

"He starts chest-bumping me. 'God,
you're such a bitch. I could kill you right now.'"

Before there were drugs, there was music. When she listens to music, anxiety disappears. Depression fades. A warm sensation settles over her body.

"Music is a huge part of my life and a major coping skill for dealing with stress," says Jennifer, a thirty-two-year-old brunette and classically trained musician with an endearing smile. "When I put music on, I feel like everything makes sense and that I'll be OK."

In fourth grade, Jennifer joined the band at her school in Elmhurst, Illinois, a suburb of Chicago. She played the clarinet.

"As soon as I picked it up, I could play it," she says. "I could make it sound beautiful."

The teacher took notice of Jennifer's talent and would have her demonstrate the assigned music to the class.

Four years later, in 1995, Jennifer's mom took her to hear the Chicago Symphony Orchestra perform Mozart's *Clarinet Concerto*. "I just remember getting all tingly with goosebumps through my body," Jennifer recalls. "Just being in awe and thinking, Wow, I'd really like to play in a place like this someday. It made me feel kind of overwhelmed with beauty. I've been to the symphony several times, and every time, I cry."

In middle school, she practiced three hours a day and was first chair in the school band. As she became a more seasoned musician, her favorite pieces to play were Dvorak's *New World Symphony* and Ferruccio Busoni's *Concertino Opus 38*. Later she would find punk rock.

Jennifer had a rough early childhood. Her parents divorced when she was one. Her biological father raped her two years later. It was her first memory.

Her mom took her to the Department of Children and Family Services to investigate what happened.

"Every time they took me for an exam, I'd hide underneath the doctor's office table," Jennifer remembers. "And no one could touch me. But I have memories of things being stuck inside of me." The incident caused a lifelong problem with post-traumatic stress disorder.

Despite the experience, Jennifer describes herself as a happy-go-lucky kid. When she was ten, she worked on a horse farm, grooming the animals in exchange for free riding lessons. She enjoyed picking flowers and going on the swings at the park. At school, she got A's and B's and excelled at literature and spelling.

Then came her first drink: a glass of champagne at a family wedding when she was eight.

"I loved it. It made me feel all funny," Jennifer says. "And everyone around me was drinking, so I thought I was cool 'cause I was drinking too."

As a tween, Jennifer listened to bubblegum pop like Debbie Gibson and Tiffany. Her stepdad — whom she now refers to as just Dad — played less-disposable rock like R.E.M. and The Police.

But it was punk that really spoke to her. When she was fifteen, she started frequenting the seedy Fireside Bowl, considered to be the CBGB of Chicago and attractive to the counterculture crowd for the five-dollar all-ages shows.

"I always felt kind of different from everybody else, but when I was at the Fireside, I didn't feel different," she says. "It was such a shithole, but it felt so cool and I felt like a badass, like I was doing something really special." She was. It was the '90s punk renaissance.

At the Fireside, Jennifer and her friend Sarah took in punk and ska bands like the Suicide Machines, Anti-Flag, and Less Than Jake. Bigger shows at the Metro included Rancid and NOFX. The two would smoke cigarettes and hang out with fellow punks.

"I hated conformists. I hated looking like everybody else," she says about high school. "I wanted to stand out. And I felt like that was what punk rock allowed me to do."

Her parents wouldn't let her dye her hair, so she pierced her belly button and her ears — four times. She didn't get a nose ring because she thought it would hurt.

"I wasn't doing drugs at that time," she explains, "so punk was like a natural high. The adrenaline would get goin'. It was beautiful."

Her first bouts with major depression began freshman year. In the journal she kept throughout high school she wrote that she was ugly and that she hated herself every day.

"Depression felt like a heavy weight was just pressing down on me from the top of my head," Jennifer says. "It felt like there was no hope."

She was also paranoid and imagined that someone was shining a flashlight through her bedroom window in the middle of the night. She didn't tell anyone because she knew people would think she was crazy.

Next she suffered a mixed state, a term that describes a rapid alternating of mood from depression to mania. She felt there was a "dark energy" living in the corner of her room, so she'd hide under the covers so it wouldn't get her. She would cry while driving if a certain song came on the radio. She couldn't sleep. Sometimes she would lie in bed, counting her teeth, or get up and work on collages mostly made of cutouts from *Rolling Stone* magazine and black-and-white photos she had taken. The collages covered every speck of her bedroom walls.

Her parents encouraged her interest in photography. As a birthday present, they bought an enlarger and all the chemicals, and they built a darkroom in the basement.

But the depression deepened.

"I imagined hanging myself," Jennifer says, "just thinking that it would be an easy guarantee that I would die. I never acted on it, but I had it planned out in my notebook."

Senior year, Jennifer smoked pot for the first time. She was with some friends and playing with a puppy while watching *Fear and Loathing in Las Vegas,* the 1998 movie about perpetually high journalist Hunter S. Thompson.

After graduating high school, Jennifer studied music at Elmhurst College. She started smoking pot every day and got a job filing x-rays and CAT scans in the Elmhurst Memorial Hospital radiology department to fund her ninety-dollar-a-week habit.

"I would go to class stoned. I would go to work stoned. I would carry around a hitter-box with me everywhere," she remembers, referring to the pot-smoker's paraphernalia that both stores weed and contains a pipe for smoking. "It made me feel the way I was supposed to feel. It took away that nervous energy and it kinda made me more mellow and kept me from getting depressed."

Elmhurst wasn't exactly a party school, so Jennifer and her friends sought their kicks in Chicago. "We would all pile into a car and smoke pot on our way into the city," she says. "We'd hang out in this studio apartment thinking it was great playing *NFL Blitz* on the Nintendo 64." They listened to hip-hop like Dr. Dre, A Tribe Called Quest, and De La Soul.

Believe it or not, Jennifer didn't get drunk until her twenty-first birthday, unusual for most young adults, let alone someone who would go on to become a full-blown addict.

"We went to a place that had Long Island iced teas for, like, five dollars," she recounts. "It was a pint glass full of liquor with a side of Coke. You had to drink it like that — one in each hand. I had a bunch of those, and then we went across the street and my brother ordered me a lemon drop and I got some martinis."

Going forward, she would binge-drink like that at least once a week. She frequented Delilah's, a punk-rock dive bar that was an island of cool in the sea of yuppies that is Lincoln Park. She hit up bars in the Gold Coast — the Hunt Club, Mother's, Finn McCool's, and Butch McGuire's.

A guy named Tim came into the picture her freshman year of college in Chicago. Jennifer fell in love. He was even a bigger pothead than she was, and soon they were spending $300 a week on weed, in addition to what they spent on acid and mushrooms. Tim stole cash from his job at Blockbuster Video to help finance their habit.

Jennifer wanted to marry him, and even though she was only twenty-three, she felt the clock was ticking. He wanted no part of that, so they broke up.

After the split, Jennifer became promiscuous, getting drunk every night at bars and picking up guys she had unprotected sex with. She blacked out frequently. When she woke, she couldn't connect the snippets of memories she managed to recall.

When Jennifer landed a job working as an underwriter for an insurance company in San Francisco, her salary doubled. Now she had the money to buy more hard-core drugs, and she started doing cocaine in 2004.

"I felt like a million bucks," she says. "I felt like I could do anything and be anybody. I started doing a *ton* of coke every day — before work, during work, after work. It just gave me this *ooh I'm free* feeling."

She didn't think she had a problem because everyone around her — friends, coworkers — was doing it too.

Jennifer thrived at work.

"I was kicking ass," she says. "I was getting millions of dollars of premiums on the books. I was cutting business deals. I got raises — big bonuses."

Liquid lunches were an essential part of her job, and Jennifer found herself drinking all day and into the night. It didn't matter that she was drunk — she was a rock star at work.

The annual retreat only reinforced the office debauchery. Every year, her company rented a party bus and drove to Napa Valley for wine tastings. After getting drunk at the wineries, the bus returned to San Francisco to shuttle the revelers between strip clubs. She was often the only woman.

The mania surfaced that year.

"I thought I was on a made-for-TV movie," she recalls, "and I felt like, in my head, there was this narration going on. There was even background music."

The mania manifested itself in textbook ways such as impulse buys — she bought plane tickets to all corners of the country but never left San Fran — and obsessive behavior, which exhibited itself in cleaning her apartment with a toothbrush.

In 2007, Jennifer met Alex, a charming coke dealer who also had bipolar disorder. He was diagnosed. She wasn't.

Jessica and Alex did coke all the time. He encouraged her to sample the product as they weighed out one-gram baggies and eightballs for him to sell. Dealing was his only job.

"He just came over to my house one day and never left," Jennifer says. In her pre-Alex days, her budget constrained her drug use. But her new boyfriend, ever the gentleman, refused to let her pay him for coke.

And so her addiction escalated. She started doing OxyContin every day — forty dollars a pill. She went to underground parties held in abandoned warehouses and did ecstasy, mushrooms, LSD, or nitrous to the breakbeats of DJs from around the world. Because Jennifer was perpetually high, her depression never surfaced.

Alex and Jennifer got married, but the honeymoon didn't last long. The charming man Jennifer had fallen in love with soon became verbally and emotionally abusive, blaming his wife for every fault in his life. Alex abandoned her in May 2008, fleeing to his parents' house in the Chicago suburb of Naperville.

Jennifer remained in the apartment on Bayshore Boulevard, near the Hunter's Point neighborhood of San Francisco — in her words, the ghetto. Drugs became her raison d'être. After getting a $20,000 bonus not long after Alex left, she quit her job, rationalizing she could live on the money for a while. But her coke and OxyContin habit was worse than she'd realized, and the bonus was gone within a month. She was forced to return to her parents' home in Elmhurst.

After getting a new job, also in the insurance industry, Jennifer reconciled with Alex and moved in with him at his parents' house, which was close to the train station for her commute to the city. This lasted a few months, and when she had saved up some money, the couple rented a condo at Marina City, two iconic downtown Chicago apartment buildings that look like corncobs.

Jennifer started using methadone, Xanax, and Klonopin, which she acquired on the black market, in addition to the cocaine. She would go out on the weekends with friends and get drunk.

That's when crack hit her.

"That was one of my *nevers*," Jennifer says. "Like, *I'm never gonna do crack*. Alex brought it home and I let him make me hate myself so much one day that I just didn't care about myself anymore." That's when *never* became OK.

She did it once and couldn't stop.

"The first time, it was great," Jennifer says. "All the pleasure centers in my brain were activated." But when the high wore off after ten minutes, she knew she needed more. And more. In four months, the couple blew $40,000 on their crack habit.

Alex had begun verbally and physically abusing Jennifer again. On multiple occasions, he pinned her down on the bed and violently lectured her. "He'd call me whore, cunt, bitch, slut while holding me down," she says. "And he'd take ice water and pour it over me."

He would ravage the apartment, destroying dishes and flipping over the garbage can, scattering its contents all over the place. He also took her phone, removing the battery and hiding it so that she couldn't call the police on him. He stole money out of her 401K. Jennifer's not sure exactly how much, but she thinks it was somewhere between $10,000 and $20,000.

She booted him out and changed the locks. When Alex returned for his things, she tried to hand them through the door, but he pushed it open and started ramming her with his chest. She recalls the hatred in his eyes as he said, "God, you're such a bitch. I could kill you right now."

She literally kicked him out the door and soon thereafter got an emergency injunction, meaning Alex was forbidden to talk, email, text, or communicate with her in any way. If he did, he would go directly to jail. She also filed for divorce.

Around the same time, Jennifer admitted to herself that her addiction had become uncontrollable and that she needed help. She also needed to talk to someone about her traumatic experience with Alex and the sexual abuse from her childhood. At Chicago

Lakeshore Hospital, she was admitted to the psych ward when it was discovered she'd been self-harming — holding her hot crack pipe against her arm and burning herself.

During that seventeen-day stay in November 2011, Jennifer got her bipolar diagnosis. By mid-January, she'd quit drinking and drugs altogether. She finished rehab in June of the same year.

Looking back, she's grateful to finally understand why she acted out. "For so long, I was convinced I was different than everybody else," she says. "I know what I am now, and I'm able to treat the symptoms.

"If I weren't a drug addict or an alcoholic, I wouldn't have this opportunity to reframe my entire life and live by a different set of guidelines," she adds. "I'm alive. I didn't kill myself. And I don't have to live the way I was living ever again."

Jennifer quit playing clarinet when she started smoking pot every day. She didn't have the lung capacity to continue.

She found her old clarinet collecting dust in her parents' base-ment, slightly warped and in need of new keys and pads. A few repairs got it back in working condition. If you heard Jennifer play today, you'd never suspect the instrument had been neglected for so many years.

CHAPTER 17

THE DANCER

*"People were planning my funeral.
I felt agony from inside and out."*

"My music is my higher power," says Natalya, a thirty-two-year-old blond bombshell with Soviet heritage. "It saves me. Because I have trouble connecting to God. For me, music helps me breathe."

Electronic music is a spiritual force for Natalya. "When I hear a beat, a bassline, the way a synthesizer is used, the spacing-out of the four-by-four beats … I don't know why, but that's what I connect to," she says. "I connect to house music. Electronic music is what touches my soul."

Natalya was born in Minsk, Belarus, in 1982, when the country was still part of the USSR. She had a tumultuous childhood.

Her older brother, Vadim, verbally and physically abused her. "He didn't have any friends and he had a lot of physical energy," Natalya recalls, "so he took it out on me." He'd punch her in the chest or arm, or sometimes scare her by leaping out of a closet, which she attributes to her still startling easily. Vadim would later be diagnosed with schizoaffective disorder, a condition that combines the symptoms of schizophrenia and bipolar.

Her parents fought constantly. "My dad never hit my mom physically, but there was a lot of screaming and shoe throwing," she says. Her parents never divorced because, Natalya says, her father was a great dad. He'd make small gestures such as bring her candy — a luxury in the Soviet Union, which had few imports — bought on the black market.

"He was a really good father to me, but he was a horrible husband," Natalya says. "And I know he cheated on my mom all the time. I remember them sleeping in separate bedrooms."

Even worse, Natalya's cousins sexually abused her. There was touching. "I remember having very misguided feelings because I liked it," she explains. "I felt a lot of guilt and shame."

Despite this, she recalls her childhood with fondness. "I wasn't a sad child. I was happy and I had a lot of friends," she explains, adding that her favorite pastime was picking berries in the forest.

Life in the USSR had its drawbacks. After playing outside all day, she'd come home thirsty, only to have yellow water pour out of the faucet. With no alternative, she drank it anyway.

Her dad owned a garage and her mom taught piano lessons to kindergartners. Mom would make Natalya play the piano, although her daughter despised it. "I was always a dancer," Natalya says. "I wanted to dance. I wanted to play. I was more active." Natalya's mother made sure she had a proper arts education, taking her to the ballet and the theater on occasion. She thinks that had she stayed in Belarus, she would have followed in her mother's footsteps and become a music teacher, because there were so few job opportunities, particularly for women.

Natalya says there was a lot of anti-Semitism in the Soviet Union. "I remember when I was six, my mother told me, 'I have a big secret for you. If you tell somebody you're gonna go to jail.'" Her mom then told her the family was Jewish, and rather than withstand further anti-Semitism, even though they weren't practicing Jews, they would soon be moving abroad to start a better life.

By the luck of the draw, the family gained sponsorship from the Jewish United Fund to immigrate to the United States. Given choices of Israel, New York, and Chicago, the family chose Chicago, where they changed their Russian last name to something less difficult for Americans to pronounce.

At first it was tough living in America. Natalya, now in grade school, had trouble expressing her feelings and processing her emotions. Like many who are bipolar, she felt hypersensitive.

Kids at school would make fun of her. "I was shorter, fatter, and had a birthmark on my nose, so they would call me a witch," she remembers. "Plus, I didn't speak the language, so I was very different."

While they got their footing, the family was on welfare for eight months, living on peanut butter–and–jelly sandwiches, which she acquired a taste for at the free breakfast program at school. Every now and then her mom would buy Pops cereal, her favorite, as a treat.

She began to develop poor body image when she started putting on weight, even though years later, when she re-watched some old home movies, she realized she'd gained only about ten pounds. She ate loads of bananas, a delicacy that had been unavailable in the USSR.

Natalya felt self-conscious about her weight. Now a high school junior, she started going to nightclubs with her fake ID. She remembers accompanying two friends who were much skinnier than she and being jealous of the attention they got from guys. Her drinking at the clubs already showed a predilection for alcoholism.

At sixteen, she craved a way to control her emotions. "I stopped eating," she says, "and I lost about fifty pounds in six months." What started out as anorexia quickly turned to bulimia. "If I didn't binge and purge, I just felt unsafe in my own mind," she says of her eating disorder. "I just needed something to help me."

In high school, her English improved and she joined the volleyball team. "Volleyball saved my sanity, because I was not home a lot," she says. "My home felt like a dark cloud in a very scary place. We were all walking on eggshells because we were all scared of what would happen to my brother, who was in and out of hospitals." Vadim, now twenty-one, had begun experiencing auditory and visual hallucinations, and even imagined he heard the neighbors killing babies.

One afternoon, Natalya's mom and Vadim picked her up from her job at a department store. In the middle of the drive, Vadim started choking his mother, and Natalya had to fight him off to keep the car from crashing. When the car stopped he ran away, but Natalya and her mom knew he would end up at the synagogue, since he'd recently become Hassidic Jewish. They arrived to find five ambulances around Vadim, who was on the ground, bloody, with his pupils dilated. "You have to save yourself," he told Natalya and their mother. He returned to the hospital for another long, restorative stay.

Natalya didn't understand what was happening to her brother, so she went online to research schizophrenia, struggling with her still-improving English reading skills. Then a psychiatrist Natalya calls an "angel" came into their lives. He would answer their phone calls even in the middle of the night.

Meanwhile, she still enjoyed playing volleyball, but because she had lost so much weight, her coach was reluctant to put her in the games. "I was passing out because I was malnourished," she says.

Despite these hardships, Natalya was quite popular, even getting voted to the homecoming court one year. She had a boyfriend, but he didn't drink because he had gout, so she didn't drink either. It was a three-year relationship. After Natalya graduated high school in 2002 and moved out of her parent's home, her boyfriend broke up with her and she started drinking seriously, even alcoholically, chugging vodka and keeping stashes of cognac around her apartment.

Her first manic episode ensued soon after. Although she was awake for a week, all she remembers is visiting her psychiatrist to get Xanax before a trip to New York, getting ready to go through airport security, and then receiving a call from her roommate that the police were looking for her. Although she's tried to piece together what happened, all she recalls is that her psychiatrist called the authorities, possibly because she might have been talking about harming herself.

She chose to check herself into a psych ward rather than get picked up by the cops. "I remember the intake people at the hospital opening my suitcase with all its high heels and little black dresses for clubbing in New York, and they were like, 'Where do you think you are?'"

After a few weeks in the hospital, Natalya moved back in with her parents and attended Columbia College in Chicago, where she earned a bachelors in marketing. She describes herself as very grandiose and promiscuous at this time, which she now feels is a symptom of untreated bipolar. There was a lot of drinking and drug use in college. She didn't live in the dorms, but she went to clubs, drank, and did cocaine.

The heavy drinking intensified. "I remember going to class really drunk," she says. Her habit of bringing water bottles full of vodka made her notorious among her classmates.

After her second hospital stay, she relapsed on her eating disorder, bingeing and purging for two weeks. To regain control, Natalya turned to cutting. The first time, "it kind of felt like I was going to explode from within, and everything was just coming at me at once. My thoughts weren't making sense," she says. "It was like an energized anxiety attack. So I couldn't catch my breath, and I just reached for whatever — I didn't even know what self-mutilation was or anybody who did it. I just grabbed a pair of nail clippers and started slicing my arms. I didn't feel any pain at all.

"Another time I was in a parking lot and my mind was spinning so fast, I reached for scissors and started cutting myself," she says. "My mind would race so much. I literally would have to cut myself to stop my thoughts from racing." One time she took a butcher knife and sliced her leg open. "I didn't tell anyone for days because I was drunk all the time," she says. "The blood would just ooze into my sock." Although she didn't get stitches, she still bears a pronounced scar on her leg.

After Natalya graduated college, another boyfriend left her. Somehow, she found the strength to join an eating-disorder support group and start a corporate job in market research. "I was cutting a lot," she says. "I had scars all over my arms, my thighs — everywhere."

She hooked up with another guy. At first it was purely promiscuous sex, but then he became Natalya's new boyfriend. "That was the worst, December of '05 to July 26, 2006. I drank every single day, morning to night." She got fired from the market research job when they smelled alcohol on her breath and her boss saw the scars on her arms.

So on that fateful July 26, Natalya attempted suicide. "I was very depressed," she explains. "I hadn't smiled for years. I remember looking in the mirror and lighting a candle. Then I wrote a note."

She had saved up a three-month supply of the antidepressant Prozac and the anti-anxiety medicine Klonopin. She popped all 400 pills at once, and the next thing she remembers is waking up in the hospital with tubes sticking out of every part of her body. After the attempt, she was sent to the psych ward for a week, where she went to her first meeting of Alcoholics Anonymous.

Two weeks later, she relapsed again. The next three years were a repeated series of hospital stays. One time, she fell down a staircase and suffered a compound fracture in her arm. She also went to the hospital for alcohol poisoning, cutting, and mental breakdowns. During this time, Natalya moved to the Chicago suburb of Waukegan, where she was homeless for several months, having fallen out with her parents. "They were done with me and I was done with them," she says.

She went to a detox center and met Lance, who had severe depression. They moved in together. An addict neighbor introduced Natalya to crack. "I had no idea what was happening," she says. "I wanted the next hit, next hit, next hit. I liked coke, but I was begging Lance to shoot me up with heroin." She snorted the drug instead. She snorted a lot of things — anti-anxiety meds like Xanax, Klonopin, and the ADHD med Adderall. She couldn't hold down a job as a waitress because of her poor mental and physical state.

When Natalya moved to Austin, Texas, in 2007 for rehab after relapsing on her eating disorder, she decided to give AA another try. When it seemed to stick, she decided to go off her bipolar meds without a doctor's oversight, which prompted the eating disorder to roar back again.

At work, her boss commented on her weight gain since starting her job. "I really started crying," she says, recalling how proud she had been of getting her eating disorder under control, only to be shamed for the results. She went back on the meds, this time only taking one mood stabilizer.

One time in Vegas, she came dangerously close to taking a drink. "A waitress put vodka in my orange juice. And I drank it. I tasted it," she says. "I spit it out. I went in the bathroom. I prayed. I called my sponsor."

She thinks one of the biggest triggers for bipolar is drugs. Weed. It will induce breakdowns.

"I used to think that ignorance is bliss and stupid people are not fulfilled as much as I'm fulfilled," Natalya says. "They're happy with their Prada bags and their showy lifestyle. I've experienced that. In the fun part of my addiction, I was traveling to South Beach and Vegas to party." It was the early 2000s, and she'd meet celebrities like hip-hop mogul P. Diddy, boy band NSYNC, and *Jackass* star Johnny Knoxville. "But it wasn't fulfilling. It was miserable."

"People were planning my funeral," Natalya says. "I felt agony inside and out."

* * *

Natalya has been sober and stable more than three years. Now back in Chicago, she works for a major credit card company, representing them at trade shows. She's feeling better than ever in sobriety and even has creative pastimes: journaling, writing poems, and dancing to hip-hop.

"I'm passionate about the Chicago house-music scene because it's about love. It's not about ego," Natalya says. "It's about expression.

It's my sanctuary. The rooms of AA are number one, but a couple of places in Chicago and the house scene are a close number two." Even though she's a regular at some of the trendier clubs, she is almost never tempted to drink.

The few times that happened, she says, "I was like, *Maybe I should go to a meeting right now*, and I do. I'll go to a club sometimes and there's coke all over and I've been like, *I gotta go home.*

In retrospect, I'm kind of grateful, because if I didn't have my eating disorder or alcohol, I would've killed myself," she says. "I'm beginning to feel more like a woman. I was a very sick girl. My reaction to life was immature and self-destructive. It was dark and violent and selfish and reckless."

Natalya's goal at the time of the interview was to start a family and have children. Mission accomplished: She met her husband, Joe, on the dancefloor at Chicago's Smart Bar and they married in September 2016. She gave birth to a daughter earlier that year.

"My identity now is I am a channel of God. My experiences are what He would want for me to have so I can fulfill my purposes," she says. "My purpose now is: I'm uniquely useful to people who suffer like me. It's my journey."

And God is music, her savior. "It helps like a meditation. It just speaks to my soul," she says. "I'm enjoying myself when I listen to music. I smile from the inside and I don't really think about the future or the past, or where I'm going. I'm just present."

With the supervision of her psychiatrist, Natalya has gone off her bipolar meds, taking only a very small dose of Klonopin for anxiety. "I really feel like I don't connect to that girl I once was anymore," she says. "I'm basically off meds, I have a very happy life, I'm a functioning person, I laugh a lot, I have good relationships."

PART III

THE WORLD OF RECOVERY

Be of good cheer. Do not think of today's failures, but of the success that may come tomorrow. You have set yourselves a difficult task, but you will succeed if you persevere; and you will find a joy in overcoming obstacles. Remember, no effort that we make to attain something beautiful is ever lost.

— Helen Keller

CHAPTER 18

WHY SOBER IS
THE NEW COOL

Bradley Cooper doesn't touch the stuff. Nor does Eminem. Robert Downey, Jr., doesn't partake anymore. Neither did the late, great bipolar Robin Williams.

Said Cooper to GQ on substance abuse: "If I continued it, I was really going to sabotage my whole life."

Many celebrities, past and present, have successfully ended their addictions and gone on to have vital, vibrant, and sober careers. And almost every one of them was just as cool — if not more so — once they decided to go sober.

Perhaps the most prominent transformation from train-wreck addict to sober soul was David Bowie. Bowie attacked rock 'n' roll as if it were performance art. From alter-ego Ziggy Stardust to his new-wave years in the '80s, Bowie changed his identity every so often, always a step ahead of the game. And even after his death, in 2016, he remains the epitome of cool — particularly as a role model for sobriety.

For most any reason an addict can think of for not kicking their addiction, Bowie showed why being sober is just so much cooler. So next time you're about to give some lame excuse as to why you want to stay on the sauce, ask yourself, What would Bowie do? Or take a look at how your addiction is making you, like, totally uncool. Just consider the following truths, arrived at the hard way by far too many survivors like the one who's writing this.

DRUGS ARE NOT REQUIRED FOR CREATIVITY

Take the long-held belief that artists produce their best work while under the influence. Sure, Bowie's revered Berlin trilogy of albums was produced during some of his most alcohol-fueled years, but the period considered his heyday occurred well after he kicked the cocaine. During the early '80s, a sober Bowie ruled the music charts, headlined Live Aid, and enjoyed the biggest commercial successes of his career. It makes me wonder how great those Berlin sessions might have been had he not been perpetually drunk.

Genius is cultivated through hard work and dedication, not via some miracle drink or drug. If you're hoping to become the next Bowie, Basquiat, or Kerouac, you won't find brilliance at the bottom of a bottle. Bowie and his genius kin were geniuses in spite of their addictions, not because of them.

After sobering up in Switzerland, away from all the drugs that beguiled him in his adopted home of Los Angeles, a decidedly better Bowie emerged. An undeniable hit factory, he wrote and released some of his best songs while sober — "Let's Dance," "China Girl," "Ashes to Ashes," and "Modern Love," as well as the anthemic Freddie Mercury collaboration "Under Pressure."

That a drug-addled pop star could maintain his world-renowned status while sober is testament to the fact that drugs and alcohol aren't requirements for coolness. In fact, I'd argue that had Bowie not sobered up, instead of gracing us with some of his biggest hits, he might have met the same fate as Jimi Hendrix, Amy Winehouse, or a litany of other artists who died far too young, robbing themselves of a longer life and further gifts to us of their musical brilliance.

SOBER MEANS STAYING SHARP

You might be surprised at how clear and keen your head is once you've eliminated your consumption of alcohol. You can work more efficiently because you're not hung over. Your brain becomes a well-oiled machine, allowing you to be more quick-witted than alcohol dulled. Feeling — and knowing — you're sharp gives you an improved overall sense of self-worth.

I enjoy listening to music more than anything in life. Being sharp, I can concentrate on the music and get more out of it. But when I got laid off, my mental obsession with alcohol took over, superseding my love for music. Now that I'm sober again, I can relish the music and feel it pumping through my heart. And I can even follow all the plotlines on *Game of Thrones*, something I never could have done during my lost years.

As you become sober, and as the chemicals wear off and your brain becomes sharper and fitter, you can read without distraction, devouring books — which was not just one of Bowie's favorite pastimes but his definition of "perfect happiness." He reportedly had 45,000 books in his collection. His bibliophilia extended so far that he stated that the ability to return to a book was the best quality an individual could possess.[1] So stay sharp. Read. And return to those books.

SOBER MEANS LOOKING GOOD

Hey you. Yeah, *you*. You look gaunt. Pale. Gray. No color in your cheeks. All that drinking and drugging has even made you a bit jaundiced. In fact, I'd go so far as to say that you're a putrid, disheveled mess.

Instead of looking like an extra on *The Walking Dead*, if you quit alcohol and drugs, you'll start to look human again. For those of you doing crystal meth, I bet your teeth are disintegrating, but if you quit now, there's still hope you'll have your chompers in your golden years. Otherwise, it's all oatmeal and applesauce in your future — and no smiling for the camera, obviously. Sure, you can get them fixed, but it'll cost a pretty penny.

Personal hygiene takes a backseat when you're in an alcoholic stupor. During my golden drunken years, I would procrastinate showering, going days and days without bothering. Same with shaving. Thankfully, online dating doesn't have scratch-and-sniff options.

---

1 http://elitedaily.com/entertainment/personality-questionnaire-david-bowie-answers-amazing/1342995/

If you quit, you'll get out of the pattern of wearing the same dirty clothes and underwear every day, because you'll actually care about your appearance. And those dark circles around your eyes will fade — in fact, your skin will overall improve: Splotches will disappear, and a softness will return. Without the drying effect of alcohol, your skin will be cleaner and better hydrated.

Bowie looked sickly in the late seventies, the height of his cocaine use. But after getting sober and reclaiming his debonair persona, he maintained his trademark Thin White Duke physique. In fact, during his Live Aid performance, Bowie rocked the same Yves Saint Laurent suit he'd worn during the Diamond Dogs tour a dozen years earlier. And just days before his death, he was still dapper enough for *British Vogue* to do a timeline retrospective of his looks throughout the ages.[2] Fat chance that would have happened had he kept up the nose candy.

BEING SOBER IS LESS EXPENSIVE

There's a lot of money to be saved once you're sober.

Now that I'm on the wagon, I use my beer money on concert tickets and vinyl records, and I'm building a pretty impressive collection. These are items and memories I'll have for years, not just for the few measly minutes it takes to down a brew. I started collecting vinyl shortly after I got sober, noting that when I'd been drunk, I'd barely had the desire or energy to do anything even as passive as listening to the radio. Collecting vinyl has opened a

---

2 http://www.vogue.co.uk/gallery/david-bowie-style-file-fashion-history-in-pictures

whole new world to me, a hobby I can count as a healthy cross-addiction, replacing one addiction with another, more positive one.

Bowie had his own cross-addiction: art. From New York neo-expressionist Jean-Michel Basquiat to French conceptual artist Marcel Duchamp, Bowie amassed some 400 pieces of art, a collection that set records when it went up for auction at Sotheby's after his death. Sure, he had more pocket change to spare than the rest of us, but keep in mind that he had been nearly bankrupt during the '70s, the height of his drinking and drugging. When you're not sharp, you're not going to make the best business decisions. Sober, he finagled financial deals that allowed him to leave an estimated £135 million to his family when he passed.[3]

YOU'RE NOT MORE ENTERTAINING WHEN YOU'RE DRUNK OR HIGH

Wanna be the life of the party? That eightball of cocaine is going to make you lively, maybe, but also a blabbering mess. And those beers, all five or more of them, will just make you a disheveled, stuttering menace. Don't fool yourself: You're not witty, you're just drunk or high.

Bowie was a notorious boozehound on his first American tour, during which he fell off the stage drunk during a sparsely attended show in Kansas City. Hardly his finest moment and certainly something he never repeated in his sober years.

---

3 http://www.dailymail.co.uk/news/article-3396656/Shrewd-Bowie-s-family-fortune-Singer-s-smart-deal-means-135million-legacy-goes-wife-children.html

You might perceive that sober means boring, but that couldn't be farther from the truth. Bowie continued partying fiercely and fully well into his sober days. On his fiftieth birthday, in 1997, he hosted a full-on rager at Madison Square Garden in which he performed — sober — with such luminaries as Robert Smith of The Cure, Frank Black of The Pixies, and members of Sonic Youth and Foo Fighters. He kicked off the evening by declaring to the audience that they were about to get "partyfied" — and his performance delivered on that promise. Regarding the event, Bowie told the *New York Daily News*: "I had assumed, like romantic poetic heroes, that I would burn it all out. But nothing has been quenched. I'm still feeling fiery."

And there's the takeaway: Sobriety is fiery.

ALCOHOL AND DRUGS AREN'T A SOCIAL REQUIREMENT

Some people use social events as a reason not to quit — as if you need to be holding a brewski or hitting a bowl in order to make small talk. There are myriad ways around this, and sober celebs do it all the time.

Take the Golden Globes. One big difference between this awards ceremony and the Academy Awards is that servers pop open the champagne all night long. And while drinking a glass of bubbly at the Golden Globes might be alluring, many stars — like the ones listed at the beginning of this chapter — choose not to. Even J.Lo opts out of drinking, because she believes it isn't good for her skin. At parties, when there's a toast, she raises a glass with one sip of wine, and then it's back to water.

If you're invited to a dinner party, a sober you is more likely to make the effort to bring a thoughtful host gift, like a homemade dessert or small bouquet of seasonal flowers, rather than bearing a sixer of beer you bought at the corner store — because now you have the energy and the wherewithal to make such an elegant gesture. At the party, instead of alcohol, you can drink a club soda or sparkling water over ice with lime — I prefer San Pellegrino — a classy drink that looks like a gin and tonic and tastes refreshing. Because you're not drinking, you are civilized and alert, following the conversation more closely, participating in sophisticated dialogue instead of slurring your words or blurting out something venomous or embarrassing. You don't feel dumbed-down or dulled. You socialize effortlessly and are literally down to earth, not as high as Charlie on a case of Willy Wonka's Fizzy-Lifting Drinks.

In everyday life, it may be hard at first, but you can create new habits for yourself, exploring new tastes that tantalize the taste buds every bit as much as a glass of hooch would. I reprogrammed my body to enjoy Italian sodas made from scratch with imported syrups and sparkling water. Instead of getting drunk, I get hydrated.

Better yet, many of the current trendy mocktails look like their alcoholic counterparts, so you can usually avoid all the "You don't drink?" grilling you might get from walking around with a can of Red Bull. And if you do get cornered, just tell them it's part of your newfound health kick — which it is.

SOBER IS MORE HEALTHFUL

There's virtually nothing healthful about alcohol — or substance abuse. *Nothing.* If you're even the least bit health conscious, it's counterintuitive — if not downright hypocritical — to drink excessively or touch any sort of recreational drug.

Another aspect to your healthfulness is that sober sleep is the best quality sleep you can possibly imagine — deep, restorative, and rejuvenating.

Drunken sleep, on the other hand, is of poor quality.[4] While the alcohol may knock you out and make you fall asleep faster, and while you may have deep sleep at the beginning of your slumber, the effects wear off and you end up tossing and turning.

When you're drunk, you don't get REM sleep, which means you don't dream. REM is the kind of sleep you need to live a healthful, well-rested life. It aids in memory formation and allows the brain to reflect on the day. Christopher Bergland notes in his book *The Athlete's Way: Sweat and the Biology of Bliss*: "People who play the video game Tetris before bed dream of Tetris in their sleep and are better at it the next morning when they wake up. Poets who read or write iambic pentameter before they go to bed dream in iambic and write poems in their sleep."

When you sleep after drinking, your heart rate also increases, which means that parts of your nervous system are more active than they should be. As the alcohol wears off, so does your deep sleep, causing you to wake up groggy with a probable headache and hangover — not the sharpness needed to go out and rock the casbah.

Then there's the calorie factor. Alcohol is loaded with them, so you're more likely to put on weight if you drink heavily. Not to

---

4 http://www.menshealth.com/health/your-journey-through-drunk-sleep

mention those unintended side calories that come with drinking, in those late-night munchies that so often accompany smoking pot or even just staying up late to drink. No fourth-meal-at-2AM post-imbibing. So you're saving about 1000 calories a day right there.

If that's not enough to dissuade you, consider how likely you are to die behind the wheel if you're a heavy drinker or drug user: 31 percent of all driving fatalities are attributed to alcohol.[5] Moreover, drinking heavily can undermine your brain, harm your immune system, seriously impair organs (causing pancreatitis, cirrhosis of the liver, anemia, gout, cardiovascular disease, and other serious conditions), and contribute to cancers.[6]

On the Diamond Dogs tour in 1974, Bowie appeared emaciated, sickly, and coke-stressed on stage. At twenty-eight, cocaine had taken such a toll on his body and psyche that he attempted suicide. If he kept up that pace, he realized, he'd be just another rock 'n' roll cliché.

In a 1999 BBC interview, Bowie was asked if he even enjoys a glass of wine now and again. "No, it would kill me," Bowie responded. "I'm an alcoholic, so it would be the kiss of death for me to start drinking again."[7]

---

5 https://www.niaaa.nih.gov/alcohol-health/overview-alcohol-consumption/alcohol-facts-and-statistics

6 https://pubs.niaaa.nih.gov/publications/hangovers/beyondhangovers.htm

7 https://www.youtube.com/watch?v=FiK7s_0tGsg

BEING DRUNK OR HIGH DOESN'T FIX YOUR PROBLEMS, IT MAKES THEM WORSE

Some people drink and do drugs to escape. A shot in the arm or a six-pack of beer or a couple of OxyContins can be a seductive sedative. But when you resort to them, you merely delay the inevitable: facing your problems. Even if you are not prone to it, drinking and downers can lead to or exacerbate depression.[8] You're also more likely to physically injure yourself. If it weren't for drinking twenty-one beers in one sitting, I wouldn't have banged my forehead on that wooden pillar, requiring two inches of stitches and leaving an impressive scar.

If you don't like your job, you dislike it even more if you're an addict, because you dread going to work. In the morning, you hit that snooze button more than you would if you were sober, ensuring you'll be late. If you finally make it to work, rather than calling in sick once again because you're hung over, you worry about coworkers smelling alcohol on your breath or emitting from your pores — because after a night of heavy drinking, no matter how hard you scrub-a-dub-dub, brush your teeth, and gargle mouthwash, you still reek of alcohol the next day.

And although your personality doesn't necessarily change when you drink, certain aspects of it may be amplified. So if you're already ticked off at someone, you may be more inclined to confrontation if you've had a few. Anger can spike and escalate, often loudy, especially if you already have a hot temper, like my former boyfriend Jeffrey.

---

8 https://pubs.niaaa.nih.gov/publications/aa14.htm

Being high might provide a temporary escape from your relationship problems, but in the end it only intensifies them. Instead of confronting the issues, you hide from them. If it hadn't been for my intervention, I might never have realized just how much I'd alienated myself from my family, and I certainly wouldn't have had the energy to work toward becoming closer with them if I hadn't sobered up.

BETTER MEMORY

Imagine creating a near masterpiece of art. Then imagine not remembering having created it. Stephen King doesn't remember writing *Cujo* because he was in a cocaine-induced stupor when writing it.

Even if you don't drink or do drugs to the point of blacking out, substances mess with your memory. Throwing up in the hallway of my college dorm is something I didn't remember until my roommate told me the next day. Colleen pointed out that on Thanksgiving, I called her twice within the span of three hours, having forgotten about the first call. In my alcoholic state, I frequently forgot to take my meds, which resulted in poor sleep and anxiety.

It's like the old adage: "Sometimes it's hard to remember, sometimes it's hard to forget, but don't forget to remember, to remember not to forget."

Who wants to forget the best times of their life?

SOBRIETY IS ACTUALLY EASIER THAN DRUNKENNESS

Being sober is just so damn *convenient*. Because you didn't blow all of your cash on booze, you can summon an Uber since you've saved money. You don't have to worry about doing something stupid that you won't remember the next day. At concerts or festivals, I don't have to pee a zillion times. I can stake out a spot up front and keep it for the whole show, because I don't have to go back to the bar for beer every half hour.

We who are sober get up early and seize the day. We don't wait in line for brunch. We beat you to the most popular places and grab a table because we're early birds.

When you're an alcoholic, you need alcohol. You're constantly thinking about your next drink. When you're sober, you don't have that mental obsession. You don't have to schlep to the store for that extra six-pack you feel you need — and actually *do* need because of your addiction. You also don't have to risk getting jumped because you're on the street by yourself at 2AM, when it's you against the drug dealers and gangsters. You can settle in at home, content with your herbal tea or chilled Pellegrino and basking in all that time you've saved by not running around to satisfy your cravings.

You also don't have to spend time covering your ass. No more excuses for missing a party or calling in sick for work. While visiting my parents in Maui, I once lied to my mother when she said she'd noticed I was drinking more on that trip. "It's just because I'm on vacation," I assured her. (Although, truth be told, I was probably drinking less than I had been at home, simply because it was harder to hide it from my parents.) But I hated lying, particularly to my mom.

Life is so much easier now that I don't have to lie all the time.

HELPING OTHERS GET SOBER IS COOL

To show how dedicated he was to sobriety, in the '90s Bowie helped tour-mate Trent Reznor of Nine Inch Nails get sober, offering wise words and empathy. For Reznor, meeting — and performing with — his hero was an inspiration. Instead of numbing himself with drugs and alcohol, he gave up heroin and began churning out more and more music.

Other celebs have performed similarly good deeds. Notorious addict and Aerosmith frontman Steven Tyler appeared in Maui, where he lives when he's not working, to lend inspiration to drug-court graduates. He credits AA with saving his life and encouraged the drug-court graduates to keep attending AA meetings.

You don't have to be a superhero to be helpful to your fellow addicts. Service is a pillar in the AA world, so my sponsor convinced me to be a greeter at meetings. Not only did I enjoy the social aspect, even if I was little more than a glorified usher, I was doing my part to give back.

For those who know an addict, Al-Anon meetings can help you help your loved ones by fostering an understanding of what they are going through; that empathy alone can be a huge boost to someone trying to sober up. Al-Anon is also invaluable in helping you through the challenges you yourself are facing through this.

* * *

In sobriety, Bowie was grateful that he had the serenity prayer — a staple in Narcotics and Alcoholics Anonymous circles — tattooed in Japanese on his leg:

God, grant me the serenity
to accept the things I cannot change,
the courage to change the things I can,
and the wisdom to know the difference.

The tattoo was not simply a statement. It was a total commitment, something to remind himself each and every day what his sobriety had brought for him.

Just before his death, the retrospective museum exhibition David Bowie Is ... began a multi-country tour of the globe. When it comes to filling in the blank of the exhibit title, many words fit the bill:

David Bowie is ...
One of a kind.
Authentic.
Imaginative.
Transformative.
Spontaneous.
Passionate.
Beyond fabulous.
Heroic.
Sober.
And above all else, cool.

CHAPTER 19

CODA

1991

September 29: the debut heard around the world. A high school gym. A pep rally gone wild, cheerleaders sporting red anarchy symbols on their black uniforms. A mosh pit. Kids flailing to the music. And a frontman with long, dirty-blond hair screaming while playing power chords and swiveling like a cheetah devouring a zebra. This is the premiere of Nirvana's music video for "Smells Like Teen Spirit." And it's massive. Especially for me.

The video is nothing like anything I or my peers have ever seen or heard. We declare Nirvana special. The band becomes the soundtrack to my youth.

With his sky-blue Fender Mustang guitar and signature agonizing wail of a voice, Kurt Cobain will mobilize an army of disaffected teenagers, carrying the flag for the freak, the geek, and the rebel, all while capturing the essence of cool. Like David Bowie or Joey Ramone before him, Kurt has made it cool to be an outsider. To be strange. To be a weirdo. Something to be celebrated, not castigated.

I have always felt that on some level Kurt and I were kindred spirits. It is credibly and anecdotally documented[1] that he was bipolar; Kurt had a monster on his back. A monster called manic depression.

Kurt was diagnosed with ADD at a young age and with bipolar thereafter, according to an interview with his cousin Bev Cobain, a registered nurse with a background in mental health. As I noticed more similarities between me and Kurt, I was drawn in by the mythos.

Both of us had an affinity toward punk ideology and problems with addiction. When early in my bipolar diagnosis I learned that Kurt too had that condition, it somehow upped his cool-factor, fitting the narrative of the mad genius/tortured artist. Our brains seemed to work the same way, in extremes: one day we were bright and happy; the next, dark and dismal. Our moods could change with the weather, as Kurt opines in 1991's "In Bloom," off the blockbuster *Nevermind*. It made me feel special to know that I was almost as off-kilter as he was.

Both Kurt and I self-medicated — he with intravenous heroin and I mostly with alcohol and crack-cocaine — to quell our moods. To stop those racing thoughts, flip the light switch. Escape.

---

1 http://www.the-bright-side.org/site/thebrightside/content.php?type=1&id=664

Even Nirvana's sound — subdued verses and big, loud choruses — drifts between two poles. But it wasn't just the loud-quiet-loud song structure that called to me; it was the intricate way Kurt played the guitar and sang/screamed. Somehow he found perfection in imperfection. That jarring, sustained clang of feedback sounded not only natural but necessary. A crack in the voice might not have made it into someone else's recording, but on a Nirvana record, it fit right into the chaos.

Kurt's depression and frustration came across as clear as unicorn tears. The 1994 album *In Utero* is peppered with feelings of isolation, low self-esteem, and harrowing emotions. On "Frances Farmer Will Have Her Revenge on Seattle," Kurt yearns for the solace in being depressed.

There is indeed an element of comfort in being depressed. Everyone in your inner circle knows it, so they dote on you, coddle you. Loved ones just want your pain to go away, and their company is more helpful than any therapy, any medication.

Kurt Cobain was the wizard of clause, a genius in turns of phrases that abound throughout the band's catalog. He reportedly had manic work binges, writing songs with lyrical motifs and song patterns that are decidedly bipolar. And clever lyrics, like those on "Milk It":

"Look on the bright side suicide / Lost eyesight I'm on your side / Angel left wing, right wing broken wing / Lack of iron and or sleeping / Obituary birthday / Your scent is still here in my place of recovery."

Esoteric, seemingly nonsensical lyrics like these drew me to Nirvana from the start. Manic people, especially if they're also writers, make odd word associations and misbehave creatively, creating art that is decidedly deranged.

Kurt experienced the intense highs and extreme lows of bipolar. "Lithium" might just be the epitome of the description of bipolar, right down to the titular drug used to treat manic depression. The song runs the gamut from happiness to indifference to sadness, sometimes within the same sentence.

After *Nevermind* was released, the early '90s became magical to me, and the record deeply affected a certain subculture. Adherents shopped at thrift stores; flannel shirts, ripped jeans, fuzzy cardigans, retro T-shirts, and worse-for-the-wear crewneck striped sweaters became de rigueur. Indie record shops popped up faster than Starbucks. You no longer had to go to a corporate mall-chain like Musicland to get your fix.

My conversion included trading in my Marithé + François Girbaud designer jeans for hole-y Levi's. I shirked my Nike Air footwear for low-top black Chuck Taylors just like Kurt's. The dirtier and more beat-up, the better.

Nirvana shattered the reigning paradigm. The movement first emerged as something called college rock, played on college radio stations "left of the dial," and that movement — later dubbed alternative rock — has continued bubbling underground since. And though Nirvana wasn't the first to create alternative rock — give that to Sonic Youth or The Pixies in the '80s, or perhaps even to The Velvet Underground in the late '60s — Nirvana set the movement on fire and took it mainstream.

Kurt Cobain was a troubled bipolar musical genius who didn't have to die so young. Despite his mantra "I hate myself and I want to die" (which almost became the title of the album that would become *In Utero*), I believe he could have survived if only he'd succumbed to psychiatric treatment.

Nirvana's final album, *In Utero*, was the one Kurt always dreamed of making. It pounces. It pummels. It thwacks, a jolt of nitroglycerin straight to your heart. Not unlike viewing bipolar painter Edvard Munch's famous work "The Scream," listening to it you can feel the artist's pain, his melancholy and suffering, his hurt. It's the most ugly beautiful album of all time.

Seven months after the release of *In Utero*, on April 8, 1994, Kurt put a shotgun into his mouth and fired. I went into mourning. MTV played *Nirvana Unplugged* on a loop following his suicide that I must've watched a dozen times that weekend.

Nirvana opened a new world to me. Kurt's poetry, a kaleidoscope of human emotion, taught me peace. Taught me love. Taught me empathy. All words that appeared at the end of his suicide note. His music may come off like a hurricane, but in the end he was really just a frail human being with a sensitive soul.

Kurt taught me that it was OK to be not OK. How to be a creature of humility. How to be empathetic. How to respect minorities, women, and gays. How to be demure and how to rock at the same time. But most important, Kurt Cobain taught me how to be punk. And that, in the end, was what saved me from meeting the same fate as him.

CHAPTER 20

THE JOURNEY OF DUAL RECOVERY

By Kenneth Minkoff, M.D.,
assistant professor of psychiatry, Harvard Medical School

"Recovery occurs slowly, one day at a time."

The remarkable stories in this book are intended, as Conor says in his introduction, to provide a vision of hope — hope for people who suffer with mental illness and addiction, hope for their families and loved ones — that out of all the chaos, desperation, and despair these individuals have experienced there can be a happy ending.

Treatment for co-occurring mental illness and addiction works, and dual recovery is possible. That's the good news.

The bad news is that dual recovery is not easy. Recovery from bipolar disorder alone or addiction alone is a significant challenge, and recovering from two conditions at once is at least twice as challenging. But it can be done.

The principles, processes, and tasks of dual recovery in general — and dual recovery related to bipolar disorder and addiction in particular — provide a framework for sufferers to figure out how to get the needed help.

First and foremost, *hope, love, and connection are fundamental.* They can make the difference between life and death.

The stories throughout this book demonstrate the extreme mood swings, risky behavior, and intense pain and despair that people with both bipolar disorder and addiction experience. They also demonstrate how long it takes before people reach the point where they get the help they need to turn their lives around. It's not an easy journey.

If you are the one making the journey, remember at your darkest moments that there is always hope of recovery, and that whatever you've suffered, and whatever you've done to hurt yourself and others, you are fundamentally a good person who deserves love and happiness. Keep your vision of a happy, beautiful, hopeful, proud life in front of you, and get the help you need to address every issue you have, so that over time you can make progress to get there.

If you care for someone who is suffering, remember that connection provides both love and hope. So many of these stories reveal that the difference between life and hope was built on a relationship. Kelly stayed alive so her dog wouldn't starve. For others, their families or friends hung in there when they needed them most to get them to accept the help they needed. Stay connected. Stay loving. It makes a difference.

Readiness to change may differ and may vary for different problems. People often become frustrated with themselves and others when they don't just "get motivated" and "do it." This is hard enough for one issue, let alone for two. There is a common language that describes the way people normally move through issues that need to be addressed, issues like smoking, weight loss, mental illness, and addiction. That language describes "stages of change" that denote steps of "readiness to change":

1. **Pre-contemplation:** *Don't bug me about the problem. I don't want to deal with it.*

2. **Contemplation:** *I am able to think about my problem, but I'm not ready to do anything about it. I need help to keep thinking and talking.*

3. **Preparation:** *I'm ready to take a small step to change. I need help to begin.*

4. **Early Action:** *I'm working on some aspects of change (cutting down my use, for example) but not fully committed to maintenance. I need help to continue.*

5. **Late Action:** *I'm working toward stability and maintenance, but I need help to get there.*

6. **Maintenance:** *I'm stable and I'm trying to stay that way, in the face of all my challenges.*

If you're wondering what stage of change a person is in, you need to first determine which issue you are addressing. People with dual disorders like those portrayed in this book may be in different stages for different issues, and thus may move through them in different ways.

Note that it takes time (months or years) for people to move through stages of change for each issue. That may be frustrating, but it is normal and represents significant progress. When someone finally says, "I'm ready to change," they've already been working and thinking for a long time.

Further, "ready to change" doesn't always mean "I will go from no interest in changing to doing everything I should." As you can see from the stories, it is common to go only partway and cycle around before making further progress. This gets compounded even more when going back and forth between two different issues.

Recovery occurs slowly, one day at a time.

Many people believe that merely completing rehab will produce dual recovery. I am often contacted by families asking me to identify the "best rehab" in the country for their dually diagnosed loved one. In these cases, many people went to rehab and then stayed sober and stable for extended periods of time. But this is not how recovery usually works, particularly for people with dual disorders.

Here's what's vital to understand: Going into a rehab program or a hospital is just a beginning. Most people are not in good control of either their mood disorder or their addiction when they first get help. Once they start to get sober, their moods and feelings may be even more out of control than before. Conversely, going on medication for a mental illness may lead people to feel less able to connect to AA and other programs of recovery for addiction. Every day requires an enormous amount of work to learn how to manage both disorders, and it is the exception rather than the rule that people learn all the necessary skills at once.

Both mental illness and addiction are "primary" problems, and recovery requires specific, simultaneous help for each of them   .

Many people with dual disorders try to figure out which is the "real" or the "primary" problem, in the hope that if they just get to the root of it all, everything else will fall into line. This is usually not the case.

First of all, regardless of which problem came first, and which may have contributed to the cause of the other (and this can happen in either direction, as the stories indicate), once bipolar disorder and addiction are present, each one requires specific treatment.

Further, there may be other issues. Most of the people in this book had significant trauma issues, sometimes associated with eating disorders, verbal and physical abuse, and self-harm. These issues also require specific attention, and the best way to approach them is one day at a time. It is necessary to follow your recovery program for *each* disorder or condition in order to make steady progress. Addressing both problems together simultaneously, each day, is what we mean by "a program of dual recovery." Treatment rarely works perfectly, so it often comes down to basic persistence.

So what is "treatment" for each of these disorders, and how does it work? We all would love it if we could just go get fixed, whatever our problems or issues, and for everything else to fall into place after that. And while this does happen on occasion, again, it is not the rule.

With regard to bipolar disorder, for example, Conor reports that his moods greatly stabilized when he started taking lithium. That does happen. But most people with bipolar disorder have difficulty finding the right medicine and struggle with continued mood swings, side effects, and the like before they find the regimen that works best for them. That process may take years and requires multiple strategies to manage the discomfort without using harmful or addictive substances.

Similarly, most people don't realize that addiction, like bipolar disorder, is a brain disease. The brain is on the other team, so to speak, so even when you decide to get sober, your brain keeps talking you into thinking that life is really about getting high. Therefore, people with addiction need to recognize at the very beginning how much help they need so they can battle their own brain and work toward success. All kinds of tools— twelve-step groups, counseling, cognitive behavioral therapies, contingency management, and anti-craving medications — can contribute to success. So can an awareness that dealing with treatment programs (and even psychiatrists) can often be frustrating, and that it is all too easy to find reasons to convince yourself that it won't work and blow it off. Sticking with a regimen for both problems is, face it, hard work.

Managing all of that together, one day at a time, takes even more work. Don't stop getting help for one problem because the other one isn't going well. When one problem backslides, it is tempting to throw up your hands and give up on the whole thing. People with bipolar disorder might, for instance, dispense with their mood stabilizers when they are using drugs or alcohol. Conversely, it may be tempting for people who start having mood swings during early sobriety to just give it up and go back to using.

Big message: *Stick with it!* Note that Conor managed to stay on his lithium while he was drinking. In the end, this was very helpful to him. Certainly, if he is on medication he is better off not drinking. But if he is drinking anyway, he is better off sticking with his medication than being unmedicated and drinking. The risks for the latter outweigh the risks for the former.

If you are experiencing mood swings and people in AA tell you not to take your meds, don't listen. That's not their job. If you are struggling with mood swings, get more help to manage them *and* stay sober — both at once. It takes time, but it works.

Recovery isn't smooth. It requires learning a host of new skills to manage challenging feelings, thoughts, and situations. As these stories indicate, for many people getting sober and starting on meds is just the beginning of a very challenging journey. We have read as they shared their stories of significant trauma and failed relationships. Many had never managed to have a relationship or accomplish a task without being impacted by mood swings or substances. All of this requires new learning during the recovery process, and this new learning takes time, is painful, and goes on for years. The skills that are needed can be described easily, but learning to use those skills is where the challenge lies. Undoing years of traumatized thinking and poor emotional habits requires building a new repertoire of skills one at a time, one day at a time.

Recovery requires learning to ask for a lot more help than you planned; indeed, one of the most challenging skills involves learning to ask for help. As you can see, during the course of their illnesses being out of control, almost everyone winds up pushing people further and further away, because they feel too ashamed and guilty to admit how much help is needed and to ask for it directly and honestly. For dual recovery to succeed, this behavior must change.

And so, make it your business to learn to ask for help from family, friends, peers, and sponsors. You have to learn to trust a psychiatrist, and to be open and honest about what is happening with your medication so you can find a regimen that works.

Moreover, learn to ask for help sooner rather than later, so that you reach out *before* things go downhill, rather than after. This all requires building trust out of mistrust and unlearning years of reflexively pushing others away, so that you can envision becoming more self-reliant and in control.

Recovery has many ups and downs. Focus on what you are doing right, and give yourself credit for making progress. You won't figure it out all at once, but you will get there eventually.

It is easy to get discouraged, but it's crucial to focus on the strength you do have and have found, not on your failures. For people with multiple issues, it takes far more strength to make even one day of progress than it does for people with only one issue. Be proud of what you are doing. In the world of dual disorders, there is no such thing as a "chronic relapse" — there are only people who are "recurrently successful."

Pay attention to what you are doing right on any given day, and work with your supporters and allies to learn how to do it better. Most important, give yourself a round of applause (just like in an AA meeting) for each day of success, for each thing you do right, and for each small step of progress in your journey.

And speaking of rounds of applause, give yourself one for reading this book. For you, it may be one of those first, baby steps, or else a way to keep you focused on recovery and progress. Whatever the case, it is part of the learning experience that will accompany you on the road you will continue to travel.

IN MEMORIAM

My wild, rugby-playing, beer-guzzling friend Jeffrey didn't make it. He died by suicide in the summer of 2017. When he was sober, Jeffrey was a joy to be around—a happy guy with a goofy sense of humor, sunny disposition, and a smile that was wholeheartedly contagious.

Jeffrey had three passions: music, rugby, and politics. He worshipped Rush and took me to see them in 2010. He also had a soft spot for even more classic rock, enjoying the music of Lou Reed, The Doors, and Led Zeppelin. We drunk-danced in front of many a jukebox in the Chicago bar scene. We probably looked like fools, but we did it anyway when a certain song struck our fancy.

As a staunch Republican, Jeffrey spoke his mind in political debates, no matter how controversial or aggressive his stance. A few years before he passed, he retired from rugby because he had experienced too many concussions, but he and I enjoyed the sport from the sidelines, beer cans in hand, as well as Chicago-style hot dogs and beer at the booze-fueled after-parties at a gay sports bar in Boystown.

I ran into Jeffrey at an AA meeting in the winter of 2016. He had built up nearly eight months of sobriety and even made his ninth-step amends to me in the spring before he died. I'm not sure he made it through all twelve steps in the program, but he definitely got further than I ever did. He relapsed, though, and just couldn't kick the alcohol. The rugby team wore their jerseys in solidarity at Jeffrey's funeral.

SUPPORT GROUPS AND OTHER RESOURCES

The following list of notable support groups, websites, and phone numbers — organized by diagnosis and then by reputation — are sure to be helpful if you find yourself in dire straits.

ALCOHOLISM

Alcoholics Anonymous

www.aa.org

The gold standard in recovery programs. Founded in 1938 by an alcoholic named Bill W. and a doctor named Bob, Alcoholics Anonymous provides support to those in need of recovery from alcohol addiction. The book *Alcoholics Anonymous*, known by its readers as the Big Book, was published in 1939 and is one of the bestselling books of all time, having sold 30 million copies to date. The famed 12-step recovery program is practiced by 2.1 million members in 170 countries.

Al-Anon

www.al-anon.org

888-4-AL-ANON

Founded in 1951 to provide support for family and friends of alcoholics, Al-Anon believes alcoholism is a "family disease," in that it doesn't just impact the addict but also affects feelings and relationships between family and friends.

Adult Children of Alcoholics

www.adultchildren.org

310-534-1815

Since 1973, ACA has been helping adults who grew up in alcoholic or dysfunctional households. As a 12-step program, like AA, it encourages members to believe in a higher power. The group's official book, *The ACA Fellowship Text*, was published in 2006. As of 2014, there were 1,300 ACA groups throughout the world.

National Council on Alcoholism and Drug Dependence

www.ncadd.org

On the scene since 1944, the NCADD offers self-test administration to determine if you or a loved one has a drug or alcohol problem. The website features resources about addiction and how to get help, as well as a frequently updated blog.

National Institute on Alcohol Abuse and Alcoholism

www.niaaa.nih.gov

niaaaweb-r@exchange.nih.gov

888-MY-NIAAA (696-4222)

One of twenty-even segments of the National Institutes of Health, NIAAA is a go-to spot for statistics on alcoholism and is the largest benefactor of alcoholism research in the world.

DRUG ADDICTION

In addition to the general Narcotics Anonymous, many other programs devoted to specific addictions follow the 12-step model of AA, including addiction to marijuana, cocaine, crystal meth, and nicotine.

Narcotics Anonymous

www.na.org

(818) 773-9999

Founded in 1953, Narcotics Anonymous is the much younger brother of AA and is focused on drug addiction, including heroin, opioids such as fentanyl and OxyContin, morphine, and more. The *NA Basic Text*, first printed in 1983, included personal stories from drug addicts, with the most recent version published in 2008. As of 2016, there are 67,000 weekly meetings in 139 countries.

Marijuana Anonymous

www.marijuana-anonymous.org

(800) 766-6779

Cocaine Anonymous

www.ca.org

(310) 559-5833

cawso@ca.org

Crystal Meth Anonymous

www.crystalmeth.org

(855) METH-FREE (638-4373)

Nicotine Anonymous

nicotine-anonymous.org

info@nicotine-anonymous.org

(469) 737-9304

MENTAL HEALTH & SUICIDE

SAMHSA National Helpline

www.samhsa.gov

(800) 662-HELP (4357)

The Substance Abuse and Mental Health Services Administration is a governmental entity whose free helpline is open 24/7, 365 days a year. In addition to help with addiction, SAMHSA offers assistance related to mental illness. It is seen as a referral service for local programs, treatment facilities, and support groups. The SAMHSA helpline averages more than 65,000 calls per month.

National Alliance on Mental Illness

www.nami.org

(800) 950-NAMI (6264)

Text NAMI to 741741 if in crisis

The nonprofit NAMI is dedicated to helping those with mental illness. Formed in 1979, there are now more than 1,000 NAMI chapters, representing all fifty states. Goals include helping to repair family relationships and fighting stigma against mental illness.

Expert professionals at NAMI are often quoted in articles or TV spots in the media, a practice that is forbidden in AA and NA.

National Suicide Prevention Lifeline

suicidepreventionlifeline.org

(800) 273-TALK (8255)

If you are having thoughts of suicide or harming yourself, call this 24-hour support number, which is also open to those who believe a friend or family member is in danger of hurting themselves. It was founded in 2004 by SAMHSA (see above).

Depression and Bipolar Support Alliance

www.dbsalliance.org

DBSA is a nonprofit organization whose mission is to offer support to those living with depression and bipolar as well as to defeat stigma. DBSA offers in-person support groups that often take place in hospitals, as well as other support groups online.

BP Hope magazine

www.bphope.com

This glossy lifestyle magazine shines a spotlight on notable people with bipolar and is a great resource for reading about bipolar in laymen's terms.

International Bipolar Foundation

www.ibpf.org

IBPF is an advocacy group and information clearinghouse for all things bipolar. A comprehensive blog features writers from bipolar walks of life. (Full disclosure: This author is a contributor.)

Mentalhealth.gov
www.mentalhealth.gov

Mentalhealth.gov is an informational resource for mood disorders and more. Anyone can find information and FAQs about anxiety, depression, bipolar, schizophrenia, PTSD, and a host of other ailments.

Veterans Crisis Line
www.veteranscrisisline.net
(800) 273-8255
Send a text to 838255

This help line, operated by the U.S. Department of Veteran Affairs and organized particularly for American veterans, offers text and online chat in addition to phone support.

International Society for Bipolar Disorders
www.isbd.org

ISBD, formed in 1999, focuses on research and education. Its members include patients, family members, and mental health professionals. The organization hosts conferences as well as webinars on bipolar disorder and publishes the academic journal *Bipolar Disorders*, featuring peer-reviewed articles on the topic.

SELF-INJURY

S.A.F.E. ALTERNATIVES
http://www.selfinjury.com
Hotline: (800) DONT-CUT (366-8288)

Since 1986, S.A.F.E. (Self Abuse Finally Ends) ALTERNATIVES has offered treatment programs for those who cut or self-injure.

ACKNOWLEDGEMENTS

Many people were instrumental in the creation of this book, from everyone I met along my journey to those who have been by my side since before I can remember. Each of you has shaped me into the sober, happy individual I am today. But there are individuals who merit personalized kudos. My dad is the most influential person in my life. He's my bipolar comrade, and I thank him for teaching me everything there is to know about writing and how to be a gentleman. My sister, Colleen, kicked me in the ass and dragged me into rehab, and I might not be here right now if it hadn't been for her tough love. My mom is my best friend, and I thank her for always lending an ear.

Because of my nine-year-old nephew, Peter—a superstar kid who puts up with my endless enthusiasm for music and the many mixtapes I dedicate to him—I get to be the cool uncle and have yet another reason to stay sober and prove myself worthy as a role model. Hats off to my brother-in-law, Jim, for being such a good dad to him. Here's to the outstanding Jenna Rose Robbins, my editor: This book is so much better with your stamp on it. And to Angela Rinaldi, who believed in me from the beginning; you will always be my agent in my eyes. Thumbs up to New York editor Meg "Mego" Blackstone for encouraging me to put my magazine cap on. You've been a wealth of ideas. Exceptional graphic designer Ana Mouriño of Lusco y Fusco expertly designed the cover and interior illustrations. Props also go to Sara Stratton, who expertly put together the pages of this book, and to Kate Zentall, copy editor extraordinaire.

I'd like to thank Chris Woods, who heroically nursed me back to health from The Great Depression of 2008. My recovery coach, Sandra Bishop, helped me obtain my footing once I achieved sobriety. My friend and high school bipolar bestie, Erin Sweeney, transcribed many of the interviews for this book and offered editorial guidance as well as chocolate sustenance. (Erin, your homemade fudge is first class!) And of course my psychiatrists, new and old, have kept me sane, including Dr. Eric C. Schieber, in Chicago, who is also a friend and keeps my moods in check. Dr. Anna Blumenthal, in New York City, brought me out of my yearlong depression.

My thanks go to Kurt Cobain for being my muse and mentor from Above. Kurt, you taught me what it means to be punk. My addiction counselor Tony at Hazelden Betty Ford was the first person to encourage me to write this book, and I am forever grateful for his inspiration as well as his role in bringing me back to healthful, sober reality.

But most of all I want to thank *you*, the reader, for taking a chance on this oddball of a book.

ABOUT THE AUTHOR

Conor Bezane is a seasoned journalist who has covered music and pop culture for nearly 20 years. In 2007, while a producer with MTV News in New York City, he was diagnosed with bipolar disorder and shifted his attention to writing about mental health. This is his first book.

Conor has interviewed and written about the Beastie Boys, Green Day, Robert De Niro, and Kirsten Dunst among others. He has covered such major events as Lollapalooza in Chicago, SXSW in Austin, and the Tribeca Film Festival in New York City. Conor has bylines in such publications as MTV News, AOL, and VICE.

He can be reached on Twitter @ConorBezane, you can join his Facebook group @conorbezane, and his blog can be found at www. conorbezane.com.